Topics
for Today

5

Fourth Edition

Reading for Today SERIES, BOOK 5

LORRAINE C. SMITH

AND

NANCY NICI MARE

English Language Institute
Queens College
The City University of New York

HEINLE
CENGAGE Learning™

Australia • Brazil • Japan • Korea • Mexico • Singapore • Spain • United Kingdom • United States

HEINLE
CENGAGE Learning™

Reading for Today 5: Topics for Today
Fourth Edition
Lorraine C. Smith and Nancy Nici Mare

Publisher, the Americas, Global, and
Dictionaries: Sherrise Roehr

Acquisitions Editor: Thomas Jefferies

Senior Development Editor:
Laura Le Dréan

Senior Content Project Manager:
Maryellen E. Killeen

Director of U.S. Marketing:
James McDonough

Senior Product Marketing Manager:
Katie Kelley

Academic Marketing Manager:
Caitlin Driscoll

Director of Global Marketing: Ian Martin

Senior Print Buyer: Betsy Donaghey

Compositor: PreMediaGlobal

Cover and Interior Design: Muse Group

Library of Congress Control Number: 2010929132

ISBN-13: 978-1-111-03304-0

ISBN-10: 1-111-03304-8

Heinle
20 Channel Center Street
Boston, MA 02210
USA

Cengage Learning is a leading provider of customized learning solutions
with office locations around the globe, including Singapore, the United
Kingdom, Australia, Mexico, Brazil, and Japan. Locate our local office
at: **international.cengage.com/region**

Cengage Learning products are represented in Canada by
Nelson Education, Ltd.

Visit Heinle online at **elt.heinle.com**

Visit our corporate website at **www.cengage.com**

Printed in Canada
1 2 3 4 5 6 7 8 9 14 13 12 11 10

To Elizabeth

UNIT 3   # Technology and Ethical Issues

UNIT 4   # The Environment

SKILLS

Unit and Chapter Readings	Reading Skills Focus	Follow-up Skills Focus and Activities

Unit 1
  Society: School and Family
 	
Chapter 1
  Hop, Skip . . . and Software?
  Page 2
 	
  Another Perspective:
  Program to Bring Laptop
  Computers to Rural Schools
  Page 14
	• Preview reading to activate background knowledge
	• Identify and paraphrase the main idea
	• Identify details
	• Organize notes in a chart
	• Analyze reading through True / False / Inference, Multiple Choice, and Short Answer questions
	• Use context clues to understand vocabulary
	• Read dictionary entries to select accurate definitions
	• Learn about and improve personal reading strategies
		• *Critical Thinking*: Infer information from text; support answers with examples
		
		• *Speaking and Discussion*: Conduct and report results of a survey; create a committee and make decisions; agree and disagree with the opinions of others
		
		• *Writing:* Write a summary from notes; write a journal entry

Chapter 2
  My Husband, the Outsider
  Page 20
 	
  Another Perspective:
  Unwelcome In Chinatown
  Page 32
	• Preview reading to activate background knowledge
	• Identify and paraphrase the main idea
	• Identify details
	• Organize notes in a chart
	• Analyze reading through True / False / Inference, Multiple Choice, and Short Answer questions
	• Use context clues to understand vocabulary
	• Read dictionary entries to select accurate definitions
	• Learn about and improve personal reading strategies
		• *Critical Thinking*: Infer information from text; support answers with examples; identify tone and point of view; identify similarities and differences; draw conclusions from statistics and graphs
		
		• *Speaking and Discussion*: Conduct and report results of a survey; agree and disagree with the opinions of others
		
		• *Writing:* Write a summary from notes; write a journal entry

Chapter 3
  Beyond Rivalry
  Page 40
 	
  Another Perspective: Middle
  Children and Their Position
  in the Family
  Page 54
	• Preview reading to activate background knowledge
	• Identify and paraphrase the main idea
	• Identify details
	• Organize notes in outline form
	• Analyze reading through True / False / Not Mentioned, Multiple Choice, and Short Answer questions
	• Use context clues to understand vocabulary
	• Read dictionary entries to select accurate definitions
	• Learn about and improve personal reading strategies
		• *Critical Thinking*: Infer information from text; support answers with examples; identify effects
		
		• *Speaking and Discussion*: Conduct and report results of a survey; share opinions in a group; support opinions with examples
		
		• *Writing:* Write a summary from outlined notes; write a journal entry; write a composition describing sibling relationships and birth order

Unit 2
  Influences on Our Lives:
  Nature Versus Nurture
 	
Chapter 4
  Who Lives Longer?
  Page 64
 	
  Another Perspective: More
  Senior Citizens, Fewer Kids
  Page 75
	• Preview reading to activate background knowledge
	• Identify and paraphrase the main idea
	• Identify and organize details of reading in chart form
	• Analyze reading through True / False / Not Mentioned, Multiple Choice, and Short Answer questions
	• Use context clues to understand vocabulary
	• Read dictionary entries to select accurate definitions
	• Learn about and improve personal reading strategies
		• *Critical Thinking*: Infer information from text; identify the author's tone; support answers with examples; draw conclusions from the reading; interpret a line graph; interpret statistics from a chart
		
		• *Speaking and Discussion*: Develop and report on ideas with a group; agree and disagree with the opinions of others
		
		• *Writing:* Write a summary from notes; design a survey; write a composition from information found in chart form; write a journal entry

Chapter 5
  Switched at Birth: Women
  Learn the Truth 56 Years
  Later
  Page 82
 	
  Another Perspective: Polish
  Twins Swapped by Doctors
  as Babies Receive Damages
  Page 93
	• Preview reading
	• Identify and paraphrase the main idea
	• Identify and organize details in a flowchart
	• Analyze reading through True / False / Inference, Multiple Choice, and Short Answer questions
	• Use context clues to understand vocabulary
	• Read dictionary entries to select accurate definitions
	• Learn about and improve personal reading strategies
		• *Critical Thinking*: Infer information from text; agree or disagree with author; support ideas with examples; draw conclusions; identify effects
		
		• *Speaking and Discussion*: Discuss hypothetical situations; compare answers with the opinions of others
		
		• *Writing:* Write a summary from flowchart notes; write a journal entry

SKILLS

Unit and Chapter Readings	Reading Skills Focus	Follow-up Skills Focus and Activities
Chapter 6 **Are Gifted Children Born or Made?** *Page 99* **Another Perspective: Reading at Eight Months? That Was Just the Start** *Page 111*	• Preview reading to activate background knowledge • Identify and paraphrase the main idea • Identify and organize details in chart form • Analyze reading through True / False / Inference, Multiple Choice, and Short Answer questions • Use context clues to understand vocabulary • Read dictionary entries to select accurate definitions • Learn about and improve personal reading strategies	• *Critical Thinking*: Make inferences about author comments; support answers with examples; identify problems and solutions; draw conclusions • *Speaking and Discussion*: Conduct and report results of a survey; agree and disagree with the opinions of others • *Writing and Research*: Write a summary from notes; write a journal entry; write a list of questions; research and summarize information about child prodigies
Unit 3 **Technology and Ethical Issues** **Chapter 7** **Assisted Suicide: Multiple Perspectives** *Page 122* **Matters of Life and Death** *Page 124* **Another Perspective: Should Doctors Be Allowed to Help Terminally Ill Patients Commit Suicide?** *Page 135*	• Preview reading to activate background knowledge • Identify and paraphrase the main idea • Identify and organize details in a flowchart • Analyze reading through True / False / Inference, Multiple Choice, and Short Answer questions • Use context clues to understand vocabulary • Read dictionary entries to select accurate definitions • Learn about and improve personal reading strategies	• *Critical Thinking*: Compare similarities and differences; compare points of view; infer information from text; support answers with examples; draw conclusions • *Speaking and Discussion*: Create a committee to discuss ethics and consequences of decisions; agree and disagree with the opinions of others • *Writing*: Make and compare lists; write a summary from a flowchart; write an opinion composition; write a journal entry
Chapter 8 **Trading Flesh Around the Globe** *Page 141* **Another Perspective: Sales of Kidneys Prompt New Laws and Debate** *Page 143*	• Prepare for main reading by reading introductory reading, taking a survey, and answering prereading questions • Identify and paraphrase the main idea • Identify and organize details in chart • Analyze reading through True / False / Not Mentioned, Multiple Choice, and Short Answer questions • Use context clues to understand vocabulary • Read dictionary entries to select accurate definitions • Learn about and improve personal reading strategies	• *Critical Thinking*: Infer information from text; support answers with reasons and examples; draw conclusions; understand a bar graph; prioritize a list • *Speaking and Discussion*: Compare priorities; share and discuss opinions; discuss causes for transplant issues • *Writing*: Write a summary from notes in chart; write a personal position and/or opinion composition; write a journal entry
Chapter 9 **The Gift of Life: When One Body Can Save Another** *Page 161* **Another Perspective: Saving Her Sister's Life** *Page 174*	• Preview reading to activate background knowledge • Identify and paraphrase the main idea • Identify and organize details in a flowchart • Analyze reading through True / False / Inference, Multiple Choice, and Short Answer questions • Use context clues to understand vocabulary • Read dictionary entries to select accurate definitions • Learn about and improve personal reading strategies	• *Critical Thinking*: Infer information from text; support answers with examples; draw conclusions • *Speaking and Discussion*: Agree or disagree with medical decisions; conduct a survey and discuss results • *Writing*: Write a summary from a flowchart; write a position letter; write a paragraph about organ donation; write a journal entry

SKILLS

PREFACE

Topics for Today, Fourth Edition, is an ESL/EFL reading skills text intended for advanced, college-bound students. The passages in this book are original articles from periodicals, newspapers, and the Internet. Some have been shortened slightly, but none have been simplified; consequently, students have the opportunity to read actual selections from a variety of publications. The topics are fresh and timely. The issues are global in nature. Experience has shown that college-bound students are interested in modern topics of a more academic nature than is often found in ESL/EFL texts. They need extensive reading in the styles of writing and with the vocabulary that they will encounter during their university studies. This book provides them with this essential practice. It requires students not only to read an article, but also to extract information from various charts, graphs, and illustrations.

Topics for Today, Fourth Edition, is one in a series of five reading skills texts. The complete series has been designed to meet the needs of students from the beginning to the advanced levels and includes the following:

- *Reading for Today 1: Themes for Today*   beginning
- *Reading for Today 2: Insights for Today*   high beginning
- *Reading for Today 3: Issues for Today*   intermediate
- *Reading for Today 4: Concepts for Today*   high intermediate
- *Reading for Today 5: Topics for Today*   advanced

Topics for Today, Fourth Edition, has been designed for flexible use by teachers and students. The text consists of four units, each containing three chapters that deal with related subjects. Each chapter includes a second reading that relates to the topic of the main reading and provides another perspective on the subject matter of that chapter. At the same time, each chapter is entirely separate in content from the other chapters in that unit. This approach gives teachers and students the option of either completing all three chapters in a unit, in any order they wish, or of choosing individual chapters as a focus in class.

The prereading preparation before each reading helps activate the students' background knowledge of the topic and encourages students to think about the ideas, facts, and vocabulary that will be presented. The exercises and activities that follow the reading passage are intended to develop and improve vital skills, including identifying main idea and supporting details, writing summaries, developing reading fluency, inferencing, learning vocabulary from context, using the dictionary appropriately, and thinking critically. The activities give students the opportunity to master useful vocabulary encountered in the articles through discussion and group work and lead the students through general comprehension of main ideas and specific information. Equally important, the text provides the students with regular opportunities to reflect on how the reading strategies they use help them improve their overall reading proficiency.

Using a classroom-tested and time-proven approach, *Topics for Today* encourages students to interact with the text, thus promoting critical thinking and skillful, independent reading.

New to the Fourth Edition

Topics for Today, Fourth Edition, maintains the effective approach of the third edition, with several significant improvements. The fourth edition contains two completely new chapters: "Switched at Birth: Women Learn the Truth 56 Years Later" about two women who grew up in the wrong families, and "Students Dig into Sustainable Farming at a Vermont College" about a college program that teaches hands-on environmentally-friendly farming. Additionally, most of Chapter 6 has been revised with new articles and activities. Furthermore, the second reading in Chapter 9 has been replaced with the first-person narrative, "Saving Her Sister's Life," which provides an update on the first article, "The Gift of Life: When One Body Can Save Another."

The fourth edition includes new photographs as well as updated charts and graphics, which are designed to enhance students' comprehension of information presented in charts and graphs and to facilitate understanding of the text they relate to.

The aim of these revisions and enhancements to *Topics for Today, Fourth Edition* is to help students improve their reading skills and develop confidence as they work through the text, and to prepare them for the academic work they are about to encounter.

How to Use This Book

Every chapter in this book consists of the following:

- Prereading Preparation
- Reading Passage
- Reading Overview: Main Idea, Details, and Summary
- Statement Evaluation
- Reading Analysis
- Dictionary Skills
- Critical Thinking Strategies
- Another Perspective
- Topics for Discussion and Writing
- Follow-Up Activities
- Cloze Quiz

Each unit ends with a Unit Crossword Puzzle, which incorporates vocabulary from all three chapters within the unit. There is an Index of Key Words and Phrases as well as a Skills Index at the end of the book.

The format of the chapters in the book is consistent. Some activities, by their nature, involve pair and group work. Other exercises may be assigned for homework. This choice, of course, depends on the individual teacher's preference, as well as the availability of class time.

Prereading Preparation

The prereading activities vary throughout the text, depending on the subject matter. This section is designed to stimulate student interest and generate vocabulary relevant to the passage. The students should consider the source of the article, relate the topic to their own experience, and predict what they are going to read about.

Reading Passage

Research has demonstrated the value of multiple readings, especially where each reading serves a specific purpose. The students will read each passage several times. As the students read the passage for the first time, for example, they should be encouraged to identify main ideas. During the second reading, they will identify supporting details. At the third reading, students can focus on unfamiliar vocabulary as they work through the Reading Analysis and Dictionary Skills.

Reading Overview: Main Idea, Details, and Summary

In this exercise, students are asked to read the passage a second time and take notes based in part on the main ideas they identified during their first reading. The teacher may want to review the concept of main idea, note taking, and summarizing before beginning the exercise. The outline, chart, or flowchart in the Details section can be sketched on the blackboard and completed by individual students in front of the class. Variations can be discussed by the class as a group. It should be pointed out to the students that in American colleges, teachers often base their exams on the notes that students are expected to take during class lectures. When the students have finished note taking, they are asked to briefly summarize the passage.

Statement Evaluation

After reading, taking notes, and summarizing the passage, the students read a series of statements and check whether each is *True, False, Opinion, Inference,* or *Not Mentioned* in the reading. This activity can be done individually or in pairs. Students should be encouraged to discuss their responses.

Reading Analysis

The students read each question and answer it. This exercise deals with vocabulary from context, transition words, punctuation clues, sentence structure, and sentence comprehension. It may be helpful for students to read the passage again as they work on this exercise. The Reading Analysis exercise is effective when done in pairs because students have an opportunity to discuss their responses.

Dictionary Skills

The entries in this section have been taken from *Merriam-Webster's Collegiate Dictionary,* 11th Edition. This exercise provides the students with much needed practice in selecting the appropriate dictionary entry for a word.

The students are given an authentic dictionary entry for one of the words in the text. One or more sentences containing the word are provided above the entry. The student reads the entry and selects the appropriate one, given the context provided. Students need to understand that this is not always a clear process; some entries are very similar, and it could be that more than one entry is appropriate if the context is general. They should aim for the nearest in meaning rather than absolute correctness. The students can work in pairs on this exercise and report back to the class. They should be prepared to justify their choice.

Word Partnership boxes, which present common collocations, have been added from the *Collins COBUILD Advanced Dictionary of American English* to increase students' ability to use language appropriately.

Critical Thinking Strategies

For this activity, the students refer back to parts of the article, think about the implications of the information or comments they have read, and consider the author's purpose and tone. The goal of the exercise is for students to form their own ideas and opinions on aspects of the topic discussed. The students can work on these questions as an individual writing exercise or orally as a small group discussion activity. In this activity, students are encouraged to use the vocabulary they have been learning.

Another Perspective

The second reading in each chapter provides another point of view, or an additional topic, related to the main reading. The students should focus on general comprehension and on relating this reading to the primary reading. The students will consider the ideas and information as they engage in the Topics for Discussion and Writing, and Follow-up Activities.

Topics for Discussion and Writing

In this section, students are encouraged to use the information and vocabulary from the two passages both orally and in writing. The writing assignment may be done entirely in class, begun in class and finished at home, or done at home. The last activity in this section is a journal-writing assignment that provides the students with an opportunity to reflect on the topic in the chapter and respond to it in a personal way. Students should be encouraged to keep a journal, and to write in it regularly. The students' journal writing may be purely personal, or the teacher may choose to read their entries. The teacher may wish to respond to the students' journal entries, but not to correct them.

Follow-Up Activities

This section contains various activities appropriate to the information in the passages. Some activities are designed for pair and small group work. Students are encouraged to use the information and vocabulary from the passages both orally and in writing. The teacher may also use these questions and activities as home or in-class assignments.

Cloze Quiz

The Cloze Quiz in each chapter serves as a final review of the primary reading. By using a section of the chapter reading, cloze exercises help students understand that they can select the missing word by looking closely at the context. For a variation on this exercise, have students block the vocabulary words at the top of the quiz and ask them to offer other words that might help complete the sentences in a meaningful way. Students can work on the quizzes alone, and then compare their answers with a partner, or they may do the quizzes alone and have the instructor check their responses.

Unit Crossword Puzzle

There is a crossword puzzle at the end of each unit. These crosswords provide a review of the vocabulary in the three chapters in the given unit. They may be done in pairs, as a homework assignment, or as an optional enrichment activity.

Index of Key Words and Phrases

At the back of the book is the *Index of Key Words and Phrases*. This section contains words and phrases from all the chapters for easy reference. This index can help students locate words they need or wish to review.

We are thankful to everyone at Heinle, especially Sherrise Roehr, Tom Jefferies, Laura Le Dréan and David Spain. As always, we are very appreciative of the ongoing encouragement from our family and friends.

L.C.S. and N.N.M.

Society: School and Family

1
CHAPTER

Hop, Skip . . . and Software?

Prereading Preparation

1 Look at the photo and read the title of the chapter. What do you think the title means?

_____

_____

_____

2 Should elementary school students use computers in their classes? Work in a small group. Make a list of reasons for and against computer use in elementary school. Use the chart below to organize your ideas.

Should elementary school students use computers in their classrooms?	
Yes, because . . .	*No, because . . .*

3 At what age do you think children should start learning to use a computer? Discuss this question with your classmates.

Hop, Skip . . . and Software?

by Victoria Irwin, *Christian Science Monitor*

1   Jody Spanglet's seventh- and eighth-grade students at Charlottesville Waldorf School in Virginia are studying revolutions. They dissect the Declaration of Independence, delve into the French rebellion against Louis XIV, and read about the various inventors who sparked the Industrial Revolution. But this

5   study happens to be profoundly counterrevolutionary in today's cyber age: Not a single classroom in the school—from kindergarten through eighth grade—contains a computer.

    Contrast that with the B.F. Yancey Elementary School in the southwest corner of the same county, Albemarle, in central Virginia. Here, computers are considered a rich resource and are used everywhere, from kindergarten through

10   fifth grade. Third-graders working on oral history projects, for example, must first pass an online minicourse. They can then take home digital video cameras and download their oral history interviews onto the school computers, which are later made available on the school's website.

    While the computerless Waldorf school is an exception in a nation that tends

15   to embrace the technology revolution, both schools find themselves on the cutting edge of a debate about if and how computers should be introduced to children at the elementary school level. At one end of the spectrum are coalitions such as the Alliance for Childhood, which has called for a moratorium on

20   computers for students in early childhood and elementary schools. Concerns range from health issues to the need for stronger bonds between children and adults and more hands-on, active play in learning. At the other end are educators and technology enthusiasts, who believe that the use of computers at an early age—even when led by an adult—can open a child's mind to ideas and

25   concepts that will kindle a great desire for learning, and perhaps make a child "smarter." Parents and guardians stand somewhere in the middle.

    Many parents, who brag that their not-yet-three-year-old can type his or her name on a keyboard to enter a computer game, also admit to a grudging guilt that they did not instead send that same toddler outdoors to explore the

30   wonders of blooming crocuses peeking through a layer of snow. "I don't think an elementary school virtually devoid of technology is necessarily bad," says Gene Maeroff, a professor at Columbia University's Teachers College and the author of "A Classroom of One: How Online Learning Is Changing Our Schools and Colleges." "Nor do I think a school loaded with technology is necessarily

35 good, or better, at meeting students' needs," he says. "Computers can enhance education. But those possibilities become greater as kids get older, particularly at the secondary level, and absolutely at the college or postgraduate level."

Various studies show different effects of computer use in the classroom.
In the late 1990s, the Educational Testing Service found that middle school
40 students with well-trained teachers who used computers for "simulations and applications" in math class outperformed students on standardized tests who had not used them for that purpose. Meanwhile, eighth graders whose teachers used computers primarily for "drill and practice" performed even worse.

Born Digital

Computer technology is a fact of life in U.S. schools and homes. Currently,
45 98 percent of public schools have access to the Internet in their schools. And one in five students in public schools overall have access to a computer. In urban schools, that number drops to one in nine—which one technology advocate calls "not a digital divide, but a digital chasm." Today, according to the National Center for Educational Statistics, 80 percent of eighth-graders have access to
50 a computer at home. Despite tightened state budgets, efforts are under way throughout the country to make technology even more relevant to students and learning. In Maine, every single seventh-grader (of whom there are slightly more than 18,000) has a laptop computer. In April, the state will begin sending computers to all eighth-graders, too. At Walton Middle School in Charlottesville,
55 Virginia, seventh-graders are using what some predict will be the educational technology of the future—handheld computers—to facilitate writing.

But how computers are used varies greatly. Elliot Soloway, of the University of Michigan's Center for Highly Interactive Computing in Education, surveyed 4,000 schools last year and found that 65 percent of students in public schools,
60 including high schools, spend less than 15 minutes a week using computers to access the Internet. *PC Magazine* reports that, of the $5 billion spent in the past decade to get computers into schools, 17 percent was used to educate teachers how to use the computers and integrate them into the curriculum. That gets to the heart of a debate over whether computer use in school is beneficial to
65 students—or merely expensive window dressing.

Quality teachers have always worked toward finding many different paths to build basic knowledge and skills that students will need to succeed in school and life, says Becky Fisher, assistant director of the Department of Technology for the Albemarle County Schools. "Adding technology to the mix only makes
70 a great teacher even better," she says. "The issue is not whether technology is

appropriate for students—most kindergartners have already mastered more technology than existed when I was a child. Rather, it is whether our teachers are supported in a way to maximize the benefits of technology."

The Human Connection

Those who think technology in the classroom should wait see technology differently. "We strongly believe that actual experience is vital for young children," says Jody Spanglet of the Waldorf School in Charlottesville. "It is important for students to interact with one another, with teachers, and with the world—to explore ideas, participate in the creative process, and develop their knowledge, skills, abilities, and inner qualities." Nancy Regan, an administrator at the school, says: "A computer is a mediated experience. You touch the keyboard, but what happens online is not your doing. Our whole curriculum is based on human connection."

It is not that the Waldorf School eschews technology. For example, it has a website. And Ms. Regan says computers at the high school level are a good idea. Her seventh- and eighth-graders will soon be doing a report on inventors from the Industrial Revolution. To do so, they are required to use at least three resources, one of which can be the Internet. Kim McCormick, who has two daughters, ages five and eight, at the Charlottesville Waldorf School, says her family is not the least bit uncomfortable that their children's classrooms have no instructional computers. "We want them to get to know the world on a firsthand basis," says Ms. McCormick, a public school teacher. Her husband is a computer program analyst. "They see us using computers for work. But we don't have any kids' things on our computer. I have looked up butterflies for them before, so they know it can be a tool and resource. But they will learn to use a computer so quickly later. My husband, who works with computers for a living, didn't learn those skills until after college."

Going Online, Bit By Bit

Technology enthusiasts say computers should be introduced in stages. Paula White is a resource teacher for gifted students who helps integrate technology into the classroom at Yancey. White says that, at Yancey, while even kindergartners are using computers in the classroom—to count candy hearts on Valentine's Day, for instance—the teacher is the one entering the information. It is not as though children at Yancey are being plunked in front of a machine without interacting with teachers. But at some schools, lack of interaction is a real concern. A mother of three children in another Virginia elementary school says she is disappointed in the use of computers in two of her children's classes.

105 When they get computer time, it is usually in the morning or late afternoon, she says, when a teacher wants to grab some extra time at his or her desk.

    Bette Manchester of the Maine Learning Technology Initiative, which oversees the state's laptop project, says even the best teachers have a hard time incorporating the four or five desk computers that often sit in elementary classrooms. One-to-one
110 computer access changes everything. "We've made this crystal clear: This is not about technology or software, it is about teaching kids," Ms. Manchester says. The success of the Maine program, she notes, depends heavily on leadership among teachers in the state, as well as the complete integration of laptops into every school's curriculum. Training involves teachers, staff, students, and parents, and
115 started well before the computers arrived. Manchester says middle school is a great time to give students intimate access to the technology. "They are at a critical stage developmentally," she says. "These kids are learning how to learn, not simply reading to learn anymore. It's been very exciting watching them take off."

Reading Overview: Main Idea, Details, and Summary

Read the passage again. As you read, underline what you think are the most important ideas. Then, in one or two sentences, write the main idea of the reading. **Use your own words.**

Main Idea

_____

_____

Details

Use the chart below to organize the details of the article. When you have finished, write a brief summary of the readings. **Use your own words.**

Name of School or Organization	Name of Spokesperson (if given)	What is this person or group's opinion about the use of computers in the classroom?
Charlottesville Waldorf School		
B.F. Yancey Elementary School		
The Alliance for Childhood		
Columbia University's Teachers College		
Educational Testing Service		
The University of Michigan's Center for Highly Interactive Computing in Education		
Department of Technology for the Albemarle County Schools		
Maine Learning Technology Initiative		

Summary

_____

_____

_____

B Statement Evaluation

Read the statements. Then scan the article to find out if each sentence is
True (T), False (F), or an **Inference (I).** Write **T, F,** or **I.**

1. _____ Charlottesville Waldorf School has many computers.

2. _____ There are no computers at B.F. Yancey Elementary School.

3. _____ Some parents believe that computers can make a child
   smarter.

4. _____ Some studies show that students who use computers do
   better on standardized tests than students who do not use
   computers in class.

5. _____ Most public schools in the United States have computers.

6. _____ Most public school students in the United States spend a lot
   of time using computers in school.

7. _____ Bette Manchester believes it is sometimes difficult for
   teachers to use computers in class when there are not
   enough of them.

C Reading Analysis

Read each question carefully. Circle the letter or number of the correct answer,
or write the answer.

1. Read the first paragraph of the story (lines 1–7).
   a. Where does Jody Spanglet teach?

   _____

   b. How old are her students?
      1. Seven and eight years old
      2. 12 and 13 years old
      3. High school age

    c. What does Jody Spanglet teach?

        1. Mathematics

        2. Science

        3. History

    d. Why is this school unusual?

        1. There are no computers.

        2. Jody Spanglet is an excellent teacher.

        3. The students enjoy their classes.

2 Read lines 8–14. How is the B.F. Yancey Elementary School different from the Charlottesville Waldorf School?

_____

_____

3 Read lines 15–18. An **exception** describes something that is

    a. different from the norm

    b. similar to the norm

    c. an example of the norm

4 Read lines 18–26.

    a. A **spectrum** is a

        1. computer

        2. debate

        3. range

    b. What group is at one end of the spectrum?

_____

    c. Does this group want computers in the classrooms?

        1. Yes   2. No

    d. What group is at the other end of the spectrum?

_____

    e. Does this group want children to learn about computers at an early age?

        1. Yes   2. No

f. What group is in the middle of the spectrum?

_____

g. **Stand somewhere in the middle** means this group
    1. does not want computers in young children's classrooms
    2. believes young children should use computers
    3. isn't sure whether computers are good for young children

5 Read lines 44–48. Fewer students have access to computers in
a. public schools
b. urban schools
c. Maine schools

6 Read lines 83–84. **Eschew** means
a. encourage
b. avoid
c. support

7 Read lines 87–91.
a. Kim McCormick is

    1. a student at the Waldorf School
    2. a parent of students at the Waldorf School
    3. an administrator at the Waldorf School

b. Does she think her children should have computers in school?

    1. Yes   2. No

c. Why or why not?

_____

8 Read lines 103–106.
a. Why is the **mother of three children** disappointed?

    1. Her children use computers in their classrooms too much.
    2. Her children never use computers in school.
    3. The teachers do not help her children use computers in school.

b. What is the teacher doing when the students are using the computers?

    1. Working at his or her desk
    2. Helping the students
    3. Assigning homework

9 Read lines 109–110. What is **one-to-one computer access?**

    a. All the students share four or five computers.

    b. Each student has his or her own laptop.

    c. The teacher works with one student at a time.

D Dictionary Skills

Read the excerpts from the article. Then read the dictionary entry for the boldfaced word and write the number of the definition that is appropriate for the context. Be prepared to explain your choice.

1 While the computerless Waldorf school is an exception in a nation that tends to **embrace** the technology revolution, both schools find themselves on the cutting edge of a debate about if and how computers should be introduced to children at the elementary school level.

embrace: _____

> **embrace** *transitive verb* **1 a** : to clasp in the arms : HUG **b** : CHERISH, LOVE **2** : ENCIRCLE, ENCLOSE **3 a** : to take up especially readily or gladly <embrace a cause> **b** : to avail oneself of : WELCOME <*embraced* the opportunity to study further> . . .

2 Currently, 98 percent of public schools have **access** to the Internet in their schools.

access: _____

> **access** **1 a** : ONSET **b** : a fit of intense feeling : OUTBURST **2 a** : permission, liberty, or ability to enter, approach, or pass to and from a place or to approach or communicate with a person or thing **b** : freedom or ability to obtain or make use of something **c** : a way or means of access **d** : the act or an instance of accessing **3** : an increase by addition <a sudden access of wealth>

By permission. From *Merriam-Webster's Collegiate® Dictionary*, 11th Edition © 2010 by Merriam-Webster, Incorporated (www.Merriam-Webster.com).

3　At one end of the **spectrum** are coalitions such as the Alliance for Childhood, which has called for a moratorium on computers for students in early childhood and elementary schools.

spectrum: _____

> **spectrum** **1** **a :** a continuum of color formed when a beam of white light is dispersed (as by passage through a prism) so that its component wavelengths are arranged in order **b :** any of various continua that resemble a color spectrum in consisting of an ordered arrangement by a particular characteristic (as frequency or energy): as *(1)* : ELECTROMAGNETIC SPECTRUM *(2)* : RADIO SPECTRUM *(3)* : the range of frequencies of sound waves *(4)* : MASS SPECTRUM **c :** the representation (as a plot) of a spectrum **2** **a :** a continuous sequence or range <a wide spectrum of interests> <opposite ends of the political spectrum> . . .

4　It is not as though children at Yancey are being plunked in front of a machine without interacting with teachers. But at some schools, lack of interaction is a real **concern.**

concern: _____

> **concern** **1** **a :** marked interest or regard usually arising through a personal tie or relationship **b :** an uneasy state of blended interest, uncertainty, and apprehension **2** : something that relates or belongs to one : AFFAIR <it's no concern of yours> **3** : matter for consideration . . .

Word Partnership	Use *concern* with:
n.	**cause for** concern, **health/safety** concern
v.	**express** concern

By permission. From *Merriam-Webster's Collegiate® Dictionary,* 11th Edition © 2010 by Merriam-Webster, Incorporated (www.Merriam-Webster.com).

Critical Thinking Strategies

Read each question carefully, and write a response. Remember that there is no one correct answer. Your response depends on what **you** think.

1 The Alliance for Childhood cites **health concerns** as one reason why young students should not have computers in the classroom. What might these health concerns be?

_____

_____

_____

2 Read lines 27–30. Why do these parents have a **grudging guilt** about their children?

_____

_____

_____

3 Read lines 38–43. This paragraph states, "Various studies show different effects of computer use in the classroom." According to this paragraph, what factor can determine how useful computers are in the classroom?

_____

_____

_____

Another Perspective

Read the article and answer the questions that follow.

CD 1
Track 02

Program to Bring Laptop Computers to Rural Schools

by Melissa Nelson, *Associated Press*

1   Beeps from computers powering up will replace the sound of books cracking open in north-central Arkansas classrooms this fall. Free Pad computers developed by a Norwegian company are being distributed to Independence County's nearly 7,000 public school teachers and students through a pilot
5   program to put technology in rural schools. The computers will replace textbooks and library books used by kindergarten through 12th graders in the county's eight school districts.

    Independence County will be the largest test site for the program, which will include 10,300 students and teachers in Arkansas, California, Hawaii, New York,
10   Utah and Washington, D.C. Bruce Lincoln of Columbia University's Institute for Learning Technology said the program represents a changing attitude about how to meld technology and public education. "It's sharing a knowledge base with people. This has been happening in some places for a long time but not in places like Independence County," he said.

15   The New York university plans to study the Arkansas project and help with its implementation. The three-year project will cost about $14 million and will be funded through corporate, private and nonprofit sponsorships, said Sandy Morgan, founder of Kidztel, the New Hampshire company coordinating the project. Free Pads, developed by Screen Media of Oslo, Norway, weigh less than
20   two pounds and do not have hard drives. They are operated through a touch screen and include wireless Internet access. Harald Grytten, CEO of Screen Media, said the computers were designed with children in mind. "All you have to do is point at the screen with your finger. A nine- or ten-year-old will intuitively start playing with it," he said.

25   The companies will begin installing the system in mid-June and plan a community forum later in the month to answer questions about the project. Morgan said each of the Independence County school districts have provided

a list of textbooks they plan to use next year. She is working with the publishers to reproduce the books electronically. "We will have filtered Internet access in the same way schools already do," she said. The Center Barnstead, N.H. mother of four said she started her electronic textbook company after noticing that her son, who had a learning disability, was drawn to the computer. "When he was on the computer or playing a video game, he was able to focus and stay on task," she said. "We have a generation of nonreaders and I became convinced that schools would be the place where the electronic book market would break."

Guy Santucci, superintendent of the 550-student Newark School District in Independence County, said several students come to his office each day asking when the computers will arrive. Santucci said the project will help link the mountainous enclaves of rural Arkansas with the rest of the world. "When kids from here go to L.A., Chicago, Detroit or New York, they are at a disadvantage not just socially but globally. With a laptop they can go to all these places."

While kids have largely embraced the project, some teachers are concerned about the changes, he said. "It can be intimidating for them, but they have to buy into the technological age," he said. "We are going to do whatever we have to do to make this work because it's a $14 million project and we aren't having to pay anything." Santucci has sold the project to teachers and parents in part by telling them it could be part of the answer to school consolidation.

Arkansas is under a state Supreme Court mandate to overhaul a public education system that the court has declared inadequate and inequitable. Experts have estimated the cost of changes at $1 billion a year and some, including Gov. Mike Huckabee, have suggested finding the money through consolidating small school districts. Santucci said the technology, which includes videoconferencing, will allow school districts to share teachers in shortage subjects such as upper-level math and science. Morgan agreed. "We are hoping to be one of the major solutions to the problems Arkansas educators are having," she said.

Although the computers are composed of fragile circuitry, Santucci, Morgan and others said they aren't worried about the kids damaging the Free Pads. The computers, which cost about $450 each, are insured.

1 What is the purpose of the Free Pad computer program in north-central Arkansas?

_____

_____

_____

2 Why are students of this rural area at a disadvantage without this computer project?

_____

_____

_____

3 How will the technology of this program improve education in Arkansas?

_____

_____

_____

G Topics for Discussion and Writing

1 Choose one person in the article "Hop, Skip . . . and Software" whose opinion you agree with. Explain why you agree with this person.

2 Choose one person in the article "Hop, Skip . . . and Software" whose opinion you disagree with. Explain why you disagree with this person.

3 Imagine that you are living in Virginia and you have a child who is about to start school. Which school would you prefer your child attend: Charlottesville Waldorf School or B.F. Yancey Elementary School? Explain the reasons for your choice.

4 **Write in your journal.** What do you think is the ideal age for a child to be introduced to computers? Why?

Follow-Up Activities

1 Refer to the **Self-Evaluation of Reading Strategies** on page 57. Think about the strategies you used to understand "Hop, Skip . . . and Software?" Check off the strategies you used. Think about the strategies you didn't use and apply them to help you understand the readings that follow.

2 Alone, or in pairs, interview several parents of elementary school children. Ask them whether their children use computers in school. Ask them whether they are in favor of young children using computers and to explain their reasons. When you come back to class, compile your answers. Of the parents you and your classmates interviewed, how many were in favor of computer use in elementary school? How many were opposed? What reasons did they have in common?

3 Work in a small group. You are members of an elementary school committee. Your job is to set up a computer policy in your school for students in kindergarten through eighth grade. You must decide in what grade the students will begin using computers and how much time they will spend on them each day. Be prepared to explain the reasons for your decisions. Compare your computer policy with another group's computer policy. Are they similar or different? Now work as a class. Put all the groups' policies on the board. Work together to create a single policy for your school.

I Cloze Quiz

Complete the passage with words from the list. Use each word only once.

access	devoid	introduced	overall
advocate	drops	kindle	particularly
age	educators	loaded	range
bonds	enhance	middle	spectrum
debate	exception	moratorium	technology

While the computerless Waldorf school is an _____ in a
(1)
nation that tends to embrace the _____ revolution, both schools
(2)
find themselves on the cutting edge of a _____ about if and
(3)
how computers should be _____ to children at the elementary
(4)
school level. At one end of the _____ are coalitions such as
(5)
the Alliance for Childhood, which has called for a _____
(6)
on computers for students in early childhood and elementary schools.
Concerns _____ from health issues to the need for stronger
(7)
_____ between children and adults. At the other end are
(8)
_____ and technology enthusiasts, who believe that the use of
(9)
computers at an early _____ can open a child's mind to ideas
(10)
and concepts that will _____ a great desire for learning, and
(11)
perhaps make a child "smarter." Parents and guardians stand somewhere
in the _____. "I don't think an elementary school virtually
(12)
_____ of technology is necessarily bad," says Gene Maeroff, a
(13)
professor at Columbia University's Teachers College. "Nor do I think a school
_____ with technology is necessarily good, or better, at meeting
(14)

students' needs," he says. "Computers can _____ (15) education. But those possibilities become greater as kids get older, _____ (16) at the secondary level, and absolutely at the college or postgraduate level."

Computer technology is a fact of life in U.S. schools and homes. Currently, 98 percent of public schools have _____ (17) to the Internet in their schools. And one in five students in public schools _____ (18) have access to a computer. In urban schools, that number _____ (19) to one in nine—which one technology _____ (20) calls "not a digital divide, but a digital chasm."

2
CHAPTER

My Husband, the Outsider

Prereading Preparation

1 In a small group, define the term **mixed marriage.** Write your definition on the board. Compare your definition with those of the other groups. As a class, decide what you mean by **mixed marriage.**

Group Definition	Class Definition

2 Alone, think about these two questions: *What is an American? When is a person an American?* Write your responses in your journal, and think about the questions as you read the article.

3 Read the title of the article. What does Marian Hyun mean when she describes her husband as an outsider?

_____

_____

4 Conduct an in-class survey using the questions in the chart. Record the responses on the chart and discuss as a class. You will use your data later when you do an out-of-class survey on the same questions.

In-Class Marriage Survey

Total # of Respondents: _____		Total # of Men: _____		Total # of Women: _____	
Is there a "right" age to get married?					
Yes		No		Not Sure	
Men	Women	Men	Women	Men	Women
%	%	%	%	%	%
Is it acceptable to marry a person of another race?					
Yes		No		Not Sure	
Men	Women	Men	Women	Men	Women
%	%	%	%	%	%
Should a son or a daughter always marry the person the parents choose?					
Yes		No		Not Sure	
Men	Women	Men	Women	Men	Women
%	%	%	%	%	%
Should a son or a daughter marry a person even if the parents disapprove of the person?					
Yes		No		Not Sure	
Men	Women	Men	Women	Men	Women
%	%	%	%	%	%

My Husband, the Outsider

by Marian Hyun, *Newsday*

1   When my husband-to-be and I announced our engagement, people were curious about the kind of wedding we would have. He is an Irish-Ukrainian from the Bronx, and a lapsed Catholic, while I am an American-born Korean from New Jersey. Some of my husband's friends must have been expecting an

5   exotic wedding ceremony.

    We disappointed many people. Far from being exotic, or even very religious, our ceremony was performed in English by a Unitarian minister on a hotel balcony. But when my husband and I decided to have 50 guests instead of 150, we caused an uproar among relatives and family friends, especially on the

10   Korean side.

    "It's very embarrassing," my father complained. "Everyone wants to know why you won't listen to me and invite the people you should."

    "Well, whose wedding is this, anyway?" I asked.

    What a dumb question. I had forgotten for a moment that I was dealing with

15   Koreans. It was bad enough that I had decided to marry a non-Korean, but highly insulting that I wasn't giving everyone the chance to snicker over it in person. I found out after the wedding that my father was asked, "How does it feel to have an American son-in-law?"

    "My son-in-law is a good man," he said. "Better to have a good American

20   son-in-law than a bad Korean one."

    He hadn't always felt that way. For years, he ignored the non-Koreans I was dating—it took him about a year to remember my husband's name. But when I was a freshman in college, I dated my father's dream of a son-in-law, David, an American-born Korean from a respected family, who was doing brilliantly at

25   Harvard and had plans for law school. When the relationship ended, my father preferred not to acknowledge the fact.

    When it became clear that David would never be his son-in-law, my father started dropping hints at the dinner table about some handsome and delightful young doctor working for him, who was right off the plane from Seoul—there

30   seemed to be a steady supply. This started during my senior year in college, and continued until sometime after my engagement.

    The one time I did go out with a Korean doctor was at my mother's request. "Please, just once," she said. "One of my college friends has a son who wants to get married, and she thought of you."

35 "You expect me to go out with a guy who lets his mommy pick his dates?" I asked.

"He's very traditional," she explained. "If you refuse to meet him, my friend will think I'm too snobby to want her son in our family. I'll lose face."

"OK, just this once," I said reluctantly. A few days later, I sat in an Indian
40 restaurant with the Korean doctor. After several start-and-stop attempts at conversation, the doctor told me I should live in Korea for a while.

"Korea is a great country," he said. "I think you ought to appreciate it more. And you should learn to speak Korean. I don't understand why you can't speak your native language."

45 "English is my native language," I said. "I wish I could speak Korean, but I don't have the time to learn it now."

"You are Korean," he insisted. "You should speak your mother tongue." A mouthful of food kept me from saying more than "Mmmm," but I found myself stabbing my tandoori chicken with remarkable violence.

50 Despite our obvious incompatibility, the doctor kept asking me out. For weeks, I had to turn down invitations to dinner, movies and concerts—even rides to visit my parents—before he finally stopped calling.

During a visit to Seoul a few years later, I realized that this kind of dogged persistence during Korean courtship was quite common. In fact, my own father
55 had used it successfully. My mother told me he proposed to her the day after they were introduced at a dinner given by matchmaking friends. She told him he was crazy when she turned him down. Undaunted, he hounded her for three months until she finally gave in.

My parents have now been married for almost 40 years, but what worked for
60 them wasn't about to work for me. I think one reason my father didn't object to having a non-Korean son-in-law—aside from actually liking my husband—was that he was relieved to have one at all.

When I was 24, he started asking me, "When are you going to make me a grandfather?"

65 And when I turned 25, the age when unmarried women in Korea are considered old maids, my other relatives expressed their concern.

"You better hurry up and meet someone," one of my aunts told me. "Do you have a boyfriend?"

"Yes," I said. . . . I had met my future husband a few months earlier in an
70 office where I was working as a temporary secretary.

"Is he Korean?" she asked.

"No." My aunt considered this for a moment, then said, "You better hurry up and meet someone. Do you want me to help?"

My husband saved me from spinsterhood. Just barely, in some eyes—I was
married at 26. We received generous gifts, many from people who hadn't been
invited to the wedding. This convinced my father more than ever that we
should have invited all of his friends and relatives. He felt this way for several
years, until one of my sisters got engaged and made elaborate plans to feed and
entertain 125 wedding guests.

As the expenses mounted, my father took me aside and asked me to talk to
my sister.

"Tell her she should have a small, simple wedding," he said. "Like yours."

Reading Overview: Main Idea, Details, and Summary

Read the passage again. As you read, underline what you think are the most
important ideas. Then, in one or two sentences, write the main idea of the
reading. **Use your own words.**

Main Idea

_____

_____

_____

Details

Use the chart to list the people the author refers to in the reading. What is each person's opinion of Marian and her marriage? Refer back to the information you underlined in the passage as a guide. When you have finished, write a brief summary of the reading. **Use your own words.**

Person	How does this person feel about Marian and the marriage?
Marian	

Summary

_____

_____

_____

_____

Statement Evaluation

Read the statements. Then scan the article to find out if each sentence is **True (T), False (F),** or an **Inference (I).** Write **T, F,** or **I.**

1 _____ Marian Hyun's husband is Korean.

2 _____ Marian Hyun's Korean relatives expected a very large wedding.

3 _____ Marian Hyun speaks Korean.

4 _____ Marian Hyun's parents have been married for more than 40 years.

5 _____ If a 25-year-old Korean woman is unmarried, she is an "old maid."

6 _____ Marian Hyun's father will pay for her sister's wedding.

C

Reading Analysis

Read each question carefully. Circle the letter or number of the correct answer, or write your answer in the space provided.

1 Read lines 1–4. Why were people curious about the kind of wedding Marian and her husband would have?

    a. Because they come from similar backgrounds

    b. Because they come from different backgrounds

2 Read lines 8–10. **Caused an uproar** means

    a. the family was very happy

    b. the family was very disturbed

    c. the family all disagreed

3 Read lines 17–18. What is a **son-in-law?**

_____

4 Read lines 37–38.

    a. **Snobby** means

        1. rich

        2. superior

        3. afraid

    b. **Lose face** means

        1. hurt your face

        2. forget something

        3. become embarrassed

5 Read lines 47–50.

    a. Why was the author **stabbing my tandoori chicken with remarkable violence?**

        1. She didn't like the food.

        2. She wasn't hungry.

        3. She was angry at the Korean doctor.

    b. **Incompatibility** means that Marian and the doctor

        1. did not get along well because they didn't have anything in common

        2. got along well because they had much in common

6 Read lines 53–58.

    a. What is another expression to indicate that Marian's father showed **dogged persistence** in courting Marian's mother?

_____

b. These terms mean that Marian's father

1. was shy about trying to date her mother
2. pursued her mother insistently
3. let her mother call him for dates

7 Read lines 80–82. Why does Marian's father ask her to tell her sister **she should have a small, simple wedding, like yours?**

_____

_____

D Dictionary Skills

Read the excerpts from the article. Then read the dictionary entry for the boldfaced word and write the number of the definition that is appropriate for the context. Be prepared to explain your choice.

1 When the relationship with David ended, my father preferred not to **acknowledge** the fact.

acknowledge: _____

> **acknowledge** **1** : to recognize the rights, authority, or status of **2** : to disclose knowledge of or agreement with **3** **a** : to express gratitude or obligation for <acknowledge a gift> **b** : to take notice of <failed to acknowledge my greeting> **c** : to make known the receipt of <acknowledge a letter> **4** : to recognize as genuine or valid <acknowledge a debt> . . .

By permission. From _Merriam-Webster's Collegiate® Dictionary_, 11th Edition © 2010 by Merriam-Webster, Incorporated (www.Merriam-Webster.com)

2   When I was a freshman in college, I dated my father's **dream** of a son-in-law, David, an American-born Korean from a respected family, who was doing brilliantly at Harvard and had plans for law school.

dream: _____

> **dream** **1** : a series of thoughts, images, or emotions occurring during sleep—compare rem sleep **2** : an experience of waking life having the characteristics of a dream: as **a** : a visionary creation of the imagination : daydream **b** : a state of mind marked by abstraction or release from reality: reverie **c** : an object seen in a dreamlike state : vision . . .
> **4 a** : a strongly desired goal or purpose <a dream of becoming president> **b** : something that fully satisfies a wish : ideal <a meal that was a gourmet's dream>

3   He is an Irish-Ukrainian from the Bronx, and a lapsed Catholic, while I am an American-born Korean from New Jersey. Some of my husband's friends must have been expecting an **exotic** wedding ceremony.

exotic: _____

> **exotic** **1** : introduced from another country : not native to the place where found <exotic plants> **2** _archaic_ : foreign, alien **3** : strikingly, excitingly, or mysteriously different or unusual <exotic flavors> . . .

4   During dinner, the Korean doctor said, "You should learn to speak Korean. I don't understand why you can't speak your native language." "English is my native language," I said. "I wish I could speak Korean, but I don't have the time to learn it now." "You are Korean," he insisted. "You should speak your mother tongue." Despite our obvious **incompatibility,** the doctor kept asking me out.

incompatible: _____

> **incompatible** **1** : incapable of being held by one person at one time—used of offices that make conflicting demands on the holder **2** : not compatible: as **a** : incapable of association or harmonious coexistence <incompatible colors> **b** : unsuitable for use together because of undesirable chemical or physiological effects <incompatible drugs> **c** : not both true <incompatible propositions> . . .

Thesaurus	*acknowledge* Also look up:
v.	accept, admit, grant, recognize

Word Partnership	Use *dream* with:
v.	**have a** dream, **fulfill a** dream, **pursue a** dream, **realize a** dream
n.	dream **interpretation**, dream **home**, dream **vacation**

E Critical Thinking Strategies

Read each question carefully, and write a response. Remember there is no one correct answer. Your response depends on what **you** think.

1 Read the first paragraph. Why do you think Marian's husband's friends were expecting an exotic wedding ceremony?

_____

_____

2 What qualities do you think Marian's father looked for in a possible husband for his daughter?

_____

_____

3 What did Marian's mother mean by **losing face?**

_____

_____

4 What can you infer about Marian's attitude when she says to her mother, **You expect me to go out with a guy who lets his mommy pick his dates?**

_____

_____

5 Read between the lines. What was Marian's aunt actually saying when she repeated, **You better hurry up and meet someone?**

_____

_____

6 Marian talks about her opinion and describes how her mother and father feel. However, she does not discuss her husband's point of view. Why do you think she decided not to write about his opinion?

_____

_____

7 What is the author's tone? For example, is she humorous, serious, sarcastic, etc.? What makes you think this?

_____

_____

Another Perspective

Read the article and answer the questions that follow.

CD 1
Track 04

Unwelcome In Chinatown
She Looks the Part, but She Doesn't Speak the Language

by Amy Wu, *The New York Times*

1   When I go to Chinatown for breakfast with my parents or my relatives from Hong Kong, we are ushered to the best table, offered a variety of special dishes and treated to warm smiles and solicitous service by the dim sum ladies.

       You might think that because I am Chinese—with the standard straight hair,
5   yellow skin and slanted eyes—I would have an inside track in Chinatown. But there are hundreds of men and women like me in New York who actually get short shrift there because we're ABCs, American-born Chinese, and we don't speak Cantonese.

       Whether it's an outdoor market, a stationery store, a bakery or a restaurant,
10   the routine is always the same. ABCs are initially greeted with a smile and a friendly word in Cantonese. Then, when it's discovered that we don't understand, the word, smile, and any pretense of friendliness disappear.

       It can be embarrassing. One time, a dim sum lady asked me something after she had chatted with my father. "She doesn't speak Cantonese," my father
15   said. The woman turned scarlet. "What, you never taught her?!" she asked indignantly.

       Actually, when I was little, my parents enrolled me in a Saturday morning private school to learn Chinese language and culture. I dropped out when I was seven, after a year or two. I had better things to do on a weekend—mainly to
20   play with my American friends. I wanted nothing more than to be like them, and that's what I became. Now, in Chinatown, I pay the price.

       Tourists get better treatment than ABCs. Ladies in cheepows bow to them. Waiters fill teapots without being asked. Managers make polite chit-chat, asking how they like Chinatown. Tourists have an excuse for not knowing Cantonese.

25   Well, nobody asked, but I love Chinatown—the smells of fried noodles, the hurly-burly, the feeling of being in another world that is like a little piece of my heritage. I don't think I deserve the treatment I receive there.

A Chinatown friend says I should be more understanding. "They live in tiny rooms, in poverty," she said. "They have very little to be proud about except this language no one else understands. You're either in or out."

To them, I'm just another Americanized young person, a failure, a traitor. Sure I understand, but most of the time I'm just plain angry. It's not that I want to be accepted, just respected.

Whenever my downtown ABC friends and I want Chinese food without the insults, we go to a take-out place near our New York University dorm. The lo mein is dry and the vegetables are watery, but the cook gives us extra fortune cookies and orange slices and jokes with us in English. He makes us feel at home. Of course, he is an ABC, too.

1 Why does Amy Wu feel unwelcome in Chinatown?

_____

_____

2 Do you think Amy Wu's experience as an American-born Chinese is a typical experience? Explain your answer.

_____

_____

3 Compare Marian Hyun's experience with that of Amy Wu's. How do you think their upbringing might have been similar? How might it have been different?

_____

_____

_____

4 Apparently, neither Marian's parents nor Amy's parents raised their daughters to be bilingual. Why do you think this was so? What do you think about the consequences of Marian and Amy being monolingual? About being so "Americanized"?

_____

_____

_____

Topics for Discussion and Writing

1 Think about the people in the article "My Husband, the Outsider": Marian, her father, her mother, her dates, her husband. Marian describes how she feels and gives us an idea about how her mother and father feel. How do you think her dates felt? How do you think her husband feels about his in-laws? How do you think Marian's husband's parents might feel about his marriage?

2 Discuss the conflicts that Marian Hyun had with her family and with her dates. What were some of the causes of these conflicts? For example, were they parent-child disagreements? Were they the result of cultural differences?

3 In this chapter, we read that Marian does not speak Korean and Amy does not speak Cantonese. Why didn't they learn these languages? Do you think they should be able to speak them? Explain your answer.

4 Think about your initial answers to the questions: *When is a person an American? What is an American?* Do you think any differently after reading the two articles in this chapter? In small groups, discuss your responses. Do you have similar ideas?

5 **Write in your journal.** Marian did not follow her parents' wish that she marry a Korean man. What is your opinion of her decision?

Follow-up Activities

1 Refer to the **Self-Evaluation of Reading Strategies** on page 57. Think about the strategies you used to understand "My Husband, the Outsider." Check off the strategies you used. Think about the strategies you didn't use, and apply them to help you understand the readings that follow.

2 Alone, or in pairs, interview several people using the chart below. When you return to class, compile your data, using the chart on the next page.

The purpose of this survey is to collect data regarding people's opinions about marriage.

Marriage/Nationality Survey

Questions	#1	#2	#3	#4
a. Interviewee is Male/Female (circle one)	M/F	M/F	M/F	M/F
b. Age: under 20, 20–30, 30–40, 40–50, 50+				
c. What nationality are you?				
1. Is there a "right" age to get married?				
2. If you answered "Yes" to #1, is the right age the same for men and women?				
3. Is it acceptable for someone to marry a person of another race?				
4. Should a son or a daughter always marry the person the parents choose?				
5. Should a son or a daughter marry a person even if the parents disapprove of the person?				
6. What is an American?				
#1.				
#2.				
#3.				
#4.				

Compiled Survey Data

Total # of Respondents: _____	Total # of Men: _____	Total # of Women: _____

Is there a "right" age to get married?

Yes		No		Not Sure	
Men	Women	Men	Women	Men	Women
%	%	%	%	%	%

Is it acceptable to marry a person of another race?

Yes		No		Not Sure	
Men	Women	Men	Women	Men	Women
%	%	%	%	%	%

Should a son or a daughter always marry the person the parents choose?

Yes		No		Not Sure	
Men	Women	Men	Women	Men	Women
%	%	%	%	%	%

Should a son or a daughter marry a person even if the parents disapprove of the person?

Yes		No		Not Sure	
Men	Women	Men	Women	Men	Women
%	%	%	%	%	%

3 a. Refer to your data. What percent of people would probably approve of Marian's decision to marry a non-Korean? Was there a difference in the responses of men and women? If so, what were the differences? Why do you think men and women responded differently?

_____

_____

_____

b. When *is* a person an American? What *is* an American? Compare your class responses with those of your interviewees. Are they the same or different?

_____

_____

_____

4 The following chart shows the number of people of various races who got married in the United States to a person of another race. These statistics compare the years 1970 and 2008. Look at the chart carefully, and answer the questions that follow.

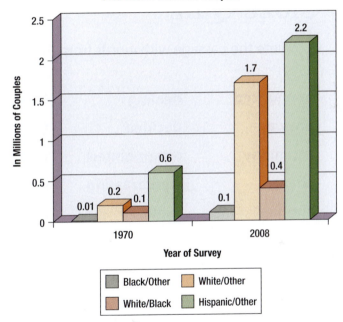

Interracial Married Couples in the U.S.

a. Which race has the highest number of interracial marriages?

_____

b. Which is higher, the number of black people married to a person of a different race, or the number of white people married to a person of a different race?

_____

c. Which race had the lowest number of interracial marriages in 1970?

_____

d. Which race had the lowest number of interracial marriages in 2008?

_____

e. What conclusions can you draw from this chart about interracial marriages in the United States? Discuss your conclusions as a class.

_____

_____

 I

Cloze Quiz

Complete the passage with words from the list. Use each word only once.

announced	dealing	father	invite
anyway	decided	forgotten	lapsed
ceremony	disappointed	friends	minister
chance	embarrassing	husband	son-in-law
curious	exotic	insulting	uproar

When my husband-to-be and I _____ our engagement,
(1)
people were _____ about the kind of wedding we would have.
(2)
He is an Irish-Ukrainian from the Bronx, and a _____ Catholic,
(3)
while I am an American born Korean from New Jersey. Some of my husband's
_____ must have been expecting an _____
(4)   (5)
wedding ceremony.

We _____ (6) many people. Far from being exotic, or even very religious, our _____ (7) was performed in English by a Unitarian _____ (8) on a hotel balcony. But when my _____ (9) and I decided to have 50 guests instead of 150, we caused an _____ (10) among relatives and family friends, especially on the Korean side.

"It's very _____ (11) ," my father complained. "Everyone wants to know why you won't listen to me and _____ (12) the people you should."

"Well, whose wedding is this, _____ (13) ?" I asked.

What a dumb question. I had _____ (14) for a moment that I was _____ (15) with Koreans. It was bad enough that I had _____ (16) to marry a non-Korean, but highly _____ (17) that I wasn't giving everyone the _____ (18) to snicker over it in person. I found out after the wedding that my _____ (19) was asked, "How does it feel to have an American son-in-law?"

"My _____ (20) is a good man," he said. "Better to have a good American son-in-law than a bad Korean one."

CHAPTER 3

Beyond Rivalry

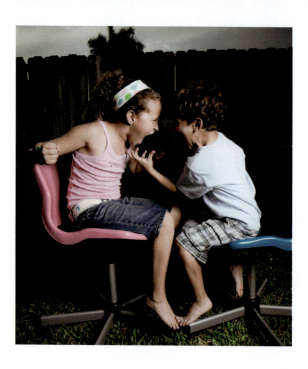

Prereading Preparation

Work in small groups to discuss the following questions.

1. How did you get along with your brothers and sisters when you were children? Which sibling did you get along with the best? If you are an only child, what kind of relationship do you think you would have had with a sibling? Why?

2. What kind of relationship do you have now with your brothers and sisters?

3. What happens to the relationship between siblings as they get older? Do they feel closer to each other? Why do you think so?

4. Of the following pairs of siblings, which do you think is usually the closest for most people? Why do you think so?
   a. A brother and a sister
   b. Two sisters
   c. Two brothers

5. Read the title of this article. What aspect of sibling relationships do you think the writer will focus on?

6. Do an in-class survey of the questions you discussed. When you are finished, compile your data. You will use this information later to compare your responses with the responses of the people you will interview outside the class.

Sibling Survey					
Questions	#1	#2	#3	#4
1. How many brothers and sisters do you have?				
2. Where are you in terms of birth order (the oldest, the middle child, the youngest)?				
3. As a child, how well did you get along with your siblings? very well OK not very well badly				
4. Which sibling did you get along with the best?				
5. How do you get along with your siblings today? very well OK not very well badly				
6. Of the following pairs of siblings, which pair do you think is usually the closest? a. A brother and a sister b. Two sisters c. Two brothers				
7. Which person in your family usually takes responsibility for getting family members together?				

CD 1
Track 05

Beyond Rivalry

by Elizabeth Stark, *Psychology Today*

1   During childhood, sisters and brothers are a major part of each other's lives, for better or for worse. As adults they may drift apart as they become involved in their own careers, marriages and families. But in later life, with retirement, an empty nest, and parents and sometimes spouses gone, brothers and sisters often

5   turn back to each other for a special affinity and link to the past.

"In the stressful, fast-paced world we live in, the sibling relationship becomes for many the only intimate connection that seems to last," says psychologist Michael Kahn of the University of Hartford. Friends and neighbors may move away, former coworkers are forgotten, marriages break up, but no matter what,

10   our sisters and brothers remain our sisters and brothers.

This late-life bond may be especially important to the "Baby Boom" generation[1] now in adulthood, who average about two or three siblings apiece. High divorce rates and the decision by many couples to have only one or no children will force members of this generation to look to their brothers and sisters

15 for support in old age. And, as psychologist Deborah Gold of the Duke Center for the Study of Aging and Human Development points out, "Since people are living longer and are healthier longer, they will be more capable of giving help."

Critical events can bring siblings together or deepen an existing rift, according to a study by psychologists Helgola Ross and Joel Milgram of the University of

20 Cincinnati. Parental sickness or death is a prime example. Ross and Milgram found that siblings immersed in rivalry and conflict were even more torn apart by the death or sickness of a parent. Those siblings who had been close since childhood became closer.

In a study of older people with sisters and brothers, Gold found that about

25 20 percent said they were either hostile or indifferent toward their siblings. Reasons for the rifts ranged from inheritance disputes to animosity between spouses. But many of those who had poor relationships felt guilt and remorse. A man who hadn't spoken with his sister in 20 years described their estrangement as a "festering sore."

Although most people in Ross and Milgram's study admitted to some

30 lingering rivalry it was rarely strong enough to end the relationship. Only four out of the 55 people they interviewed had completely broken with their siblings and only one of the four felt comfortable with the break, leaving the researchers to ask, "Is it psychologically impossible to disassociate oneself from one's siblings in the way one can forget old friends or even former mates?"

35 As brothers and sisters advance into old age, "closeness increases and rivalry diminishes," explains Victor Cicirelli, a psychologist at Purdue University. Most of the elderly people he interviewed said they had supportive and friendly dealings and got along well or very well with their brothers and sisters. Only four percent got along poorly.

40 Gold found that as people age they often become more involved with and interested in their siblings. Fifty-three percent of those she interviewed said that contact with their sisters and brothers increased in late adulthood. With family and career obligations reduced, many said they had more time for each other. Others said that they felt it was "time to heal wounds." A man who had recently

45 reconciled with his brother told Gold, "There's something that lets older people put aside the bad deeds of the past and focus a little on what we need now . . . especially when it's brothers and sisters."

[1]"Baby Boom" generation refers to the people who were born in the United States from 1946 to 1964, when the birth rate increased dramatically. Seventeen million children were born during this 18-year period.

Another reason for increased contact was anxiety about a sister's or brother's declining health. Many would call more often to "check in" and see how the other was doing. Men especially reported feeling increased responsibility for a sibling; women were more likely to cite emotional motivations such as feelings of empathy and security.

Siblings also assume special importance as other sources of contact and support dwindle. Each of us moves through life with a "convoy" of people who supply comfort and nurturance, says psychologist Toni C. Antonucci of the University of Michigan. As we age, the size of the convoy gradually declines because of death, sickness or moving. "Brothers and sisters who may not have been important convoy members earlier in life can become so in old age," Gold says. And they do more than fill in gaps. Many people told Gold that the loneliness they felt could not be satisfied by just anyone. They wanted a specific type of relationship, one that only someone who had shared their past could provide.

This far-reaching link to the past is a powerful bond between siblings in later life. "There's a review process we all go through in old age to resolve whether we are pleased with our lives," Gold explains. "A sibling can help retrieve a memory and validate our experiences. People have said to me, 'I can remember some with my spouse or with friends. But the only person who goes all the way back is my sister or brother.'"

Cicirelli agrees that reviewing the past together is a rewarding activity. "Siblings have a very important role in maintaining a connection to early life," he says. "Discussing the past evokes the warmth of early family life. It validates and clarifies events of the early years." Furthermore, he has found that encouraging depressed older people to reminisce with a sister or brother can improve their morale.

Some of the factors that affect how much contact siblings will have, such as how near they live, are obvious. Others are more unexpected—for example, whether there is a sister in the clan. Cicirelli found that elderly people most often feel closest to a sister and are more likely to keep in touch through her. According to Gold, sisters, by tradition, often assume a caretaking and kin-keeping role, especially after the death of their mother. "In many situations you see two brothers who don't talk to each other that much but keep track of each other through their sisters," she says. Researchers have found that the bond between sisters is strongest, followed by the one between sisters and brothers and, last, between brothers.

Sisters and brothers who live near each other will, as a matter of course, see more of each other. But Cicirelli says that proximity is not crucial to a strong relationship later in life. "Because of multiple chronic illnesses, people in their 80s and 90s can't get together that easily. Even so, the sibling seems to evoke positive feelings based on the images or feelings inside."

Gold's findings support this assertion. During a two-year period, contact among her respondents decreased slightly, but positive feelings increased. "Just the idea that the sibling is alive, that 'there is someone I can call,' is comforting."

Although older people may find solace in the thought that their siblings are there if they need them, rarely do they call each other for help or offer each other instrumental support, such as loaning money, running errands or performing favors. "Even though you find siblings saying that they'd be glad to help each other and saying they would ask for help if necessary, rarely do they ask," Cicirelli points out.

Gold believes that there are several reasons siblings don't turn to each other more for instrumental help. First, since they are usually about the same age, they may be equally needy or frail. Another reason is that many people consider their siblings safety nets who will save them after everything else has failed. A son or daughter will almost always be turned to first. It's more acceptable in our society to look up or down the family ladder for help than sideways.

Finally, siblings may not turn to each other for help because of latent rivalry. They may believe that if they need to call on a brother or sister they are admitting that the other person is a success and "I am a failure." Almost all of the people in Gold's study said they would rather continue on their own than ask their sister or brother for help. But she found that a crisis beyond control would inspire "a 'rallying' of some or all siblings around the brother or sister in need."

Despite the quarreling and competition many people associate with the mere mention of their sisters and brothers, most of us, Gold says, will find "unexpected strengths in this relationship in later life."

Reading Overview: Main Idea, Details, and Summary

Read the passage again. As you read, underline what you think are the most important ideas. Then, in one or two sentences, write the main idea of the reading. **Use your own words.**

Main Idea

_____

_____

_____

Details

Use the outline below to organize the information about sibling relationships. Refer back to the information you underlined in the passage as a guide. When you have finished, write a brief summary of the reading. **Use your own words.**

I. Social Connections

   A. _____

      1. *have careers* _____

      2. _____

      3. _____

   B. Older Adult Siblings

      1. _____

      2. _____

      3. _____

II. Effects of Critical Events in Siblings' Lives

   A. _____

   B. _____

III. _____

    A. _____

    B. _____

    C. 53 percent increased contact

        1. _____

        2. *anxiety about sibling's health*

        3. _____

        4. *need link to the past*

IV. _____

    A. Proximity

    B. _____

V. Why Siblings Don't Ask Each Other for Help

    A. _____

    B. _____

    C. _____

Summary

_____

_____

_____

_____

_____

B Statement Evaluation

Read the statements. Then scan the article to find out if each sentence is **True (T)**, **False (F)**, or **Not Mentioned (NM)** in the article. Write **T, F,** or **NM.**

1 _____ Critical events always bring siblings closer together.

2 _____ Most older people are angry or hostile towards their siblings.

3 _____ Many brothers and sisters have more contact with each other as they age.

4 _____ Older male siblings argue more than older female siblings do.

5 _____ Older brothers and sisters enjoy talking together about the past.

6 _____ The age difference between siblings is an important factor in sibling rivalry.

7 _____ Older people prefer to call their siblings for help instead of their children.

C Reading Analysis

Read each question carefully. Circle the letter or number of the correct answer, or write the answer.

1 Read lines 18–23.

   a. Critical events can bring siblings together or deepen an existing rift. This sentence means that critical events

   1. can have opposite effects on siblings
   2. always make siblings feel closer
   3. always pull siblings apart

   b. What are examples of **critical events** in the paragraph?

   _____

2 Read lines 27–28.

    a. What is an **estrangement?**

        1. A family
        2. A closeness
        3. A separation

    b. How do you know?

    _____

    _____

3 Read lines 29–34. Why did the researchers ask this question?

    a. The majority of the people in the study did not have contact with their siblings. The researchers wondered why.

    b. The majority of the people in the study had contact with their siblings. The researchers wondered why.

4 Read lines 35–36. The authors state that **closeness increases and rivalry diminishes. Diminishes** is

    a. a synonym of increases
    b. an antonym of increases

5 Read lines 53–58.

    a. Which word in this paragraph is a synonym of **dwindle?**

    _____

    b. What is a **convoy** of people?

    _____

    _____

    c. **Brothers and sisters who may not have been important convoy members earlier in life can become so in old age.** In this sentence, **so** means

        1. important convoy members
        2. as a result
        3. very

6 Read lines 66–67. What is the meaning of **all the way back?**

_____

7 Read lines 73–78.

   a. What is the meaning of **clan?**

      1. Family
      2. Old people
      3. Hospital

   b. What is the meaning of **kin?**

      1. Health
      2. Communication
      3. Relatives

8 Read lines 83–87. What word in this paragraph is a synonym of the phrase **live near each other?**

_____

9 Read lines 91–94.

   a. What does **solace** mean?

      1. Sibling
      2. Comfort
      3. Anger

   b. What are examples of **instrumental support?**

_____

_____

   c. How do you know?

_____

_____

Dictionary Skills

Read the excerpts from the article. Then read the dictionary entry for the boldfaced word and write the number of the definition that is appropriate for the context. Be prepared to explain your choice.

1 But in later life, with retirement, an empty nest, and parents and sometimes spouses gone, brothers and sisters often turn back to each other for a special affinity and **link** to the past.

link: _____

> **link** **1** : a connecting structure: as **a** *(1)* : a single ring or division of a chain *(2)* : one of the standardized divisions of a surveyor's chain that is 7.92 inches (20.1 centimeters) long and serves as a measure of length **b** : cuff link **c** : bond **d** : an intermediate rod or piece for transmitting force or motion; *especially* : a short connecting rod with a hole or pin at each end **e** : the fusible member of an electrical fuse **2** : something analogous to a link of chain: as **a** : a segment of sausage in a chain **b** : a connecting element or factor <found a link between smoking and cancer> . . .

2 The late-life **bond** between brothers and sisters may be especially important to the "Baby Boom" generation now in adulthood.

Brothers and sisters who may not have been important convoy members earlier in life can become so in old age. Many people said that the loneliness they felt could not be satisfied by just anyone. They wanted a specific type of relationship, one that only someone who had shared their past could provide. This far-reaching link to the past is a powerful **bond** between siblings in later life.

bond: _____

> **bond** **1** : something that binds or restrains : fetter **2** : a binding agreement : covenant **3 a** : a band or cord used to tie something **b** : a material or device for binding **c** : an attractive force that holds together the atoms, ions, or groups of atoms in a molecule or crystal **d** : an adhesive, cementing material, or fusible ingredient that combines, unites, or strengthens **4** : a uniting or binding element or force : tie <the bonds of friendship> . . .

3 A sibling can help retrieve a memory and validate our experiences. Discussing the past can **evoke** the warmth of early family life.

Because of multiple chronic illnesses, people in their 80s and 90s can't get together that easily. Even so, the sibling seems to **evoke** positive feelings based on the images or feelings inside.

evoke: _____

> **evoke** **1** : to call forth or up: as **a** : conjure <evoke evil spirits> **b** : to cite especially with approval or for support : invoke **c** : to bring to mind or recollection <this place evokes memories> **2** : to re-create imaginatively

4 The sibling relationship becomes for many the only intimate connection that seems to **last.** Friends and neighbors may move away, former coworkers are forgotten, marriages break up, but our brothers and sisters remain our brothers and sisters.

last: _____

> **last** *intransitive verb* **1** : to continue in time **2** **a** : to remain fresh or unimpaired : ENDURE **b** : to manage to continue (as in a course of action) **c** : to continue to live
> *transitive verb* **1** : to continue in existence or action as long as or longer than —often used with *out* <couldn't last out the training program> **2** : to be enough for the needs of <the supplies will last them a week>

5 A sibling can help retrieve a memory and **validate** our experiences. Siblings have a very important role in maintaining a connection to early life. Discussing the past evokes the warmth of early family life. It **validates** and clarifies events of the early years.

validate: _____

> **validate** ▮ **a :** to make legally valid : RATIFY **b :** to grant official sanction to by marking <*validated* her passport> **c :** to confirm the validity of (an election); *also* : to declare (a person) elected ▮ **a :** to support or corroborate on a sound or authoritative basis <experiments designed to validate the hypothesis> **b :** to recognize, establish, or illustrate the worthiness or legitimacy of <validate his concerns>

Word Partnership	Use *link* with:
adj.	**direct** link, **possible** link, **vital** link, **strong/weak** link
v.	**establish a** link, **find a** link, **attempt to** link, **click on a** link

E Critical Thinking Strategies

Read each question carefully, and write a response. Remember that there is no one correct answer. Your response depends on what **you** think.

1 Why might the "Baby Boom" generation have a high divorce rate? Why might this group have fewer children than previous American generations?

_____

_____

_____

_____

_____

By permission. From *Merriam-Webster's Collegiate® Dictionary*, 11th Edition © 2010 by Merriam-Webster, Incorporated (www.Merriam-Webster.com).

2 Is there a difference between men's and women's feelings toward their siblings? Explain your answer.

_____

_____

_____

_____

3 Why do sisters often assume a caretaking role, especially after the death of their mother?

_____

_____

_____

_____

4 Why did contact among siblings decrease, while positive feelings among them increased?

_____

_____

_____

_____

Another Perspective

Read the article and do the activities that follow.

CD 1
Track 06

Middle Children and Their Position in the Family

by Dr. Kevin Leman, from *Living in a Step-Family without Getting Stepped On*

1   Middle-born children will tell you that they usually didn't feel all that special while growing up. The first-born had his spot—carrier of the family banner and responsible for everything. The last born had his comfy little role, but the middle born had no distinctive place to call his own. . . .

5   Middle-borns just seem to be easily overlooked, and maybe that's why there are so few pictures of them in the family photo album. There may be hundreds, seemingly thousands, of pictures of the firstborn. And the baby of the family will make sure she attracts enough attention to fill a few album pages. For some strange reason, however, which I have confirmed by polling middle-born

10 children around the world, there are seldom many pictures of the middle child, and what photos there are have him included with the others—squeezed again between the older sibling and the younger sibling.

Another thing that can be said of many middle-born children is that they typically place great importance on their peer group. The middle child is well

15 known for going outside the home to make friends faster than anybody else in the family. When a child feels like a fifth wheel at home, friends become very important; as a result, many middle children (but not all, of course) tend to be the social lions of the family. While firstborns, typically, have fewer friends, middle children often have many.

20 Middle children have a propensity to leave home first and live farther away from the family than anyone else. I observed a dramatic illustration of this tendency while I was a guest on Oprah Winfrey's show. The subject that day was sibling rivalry. Three charming young women, all sisters, were among the guests, and we quickly learned that the firstborn and the last born were residents of the

25 Eastern state where they had grown up. They had settled down near their parents and other family members. But the middle child had moved to the West Coast.

I suppose she could have gotten another two thousand miles farther away by moving to Hawaii, but her point was still well made. Middle children are the ones who will most often physically distance themselves from the rest of the family. It's not necessarily because they're on the outs with everyone else. They simply like to do their own thing, make their own friends, and live their own lives. . . .

All of this is not to say that middle children totally ignore their siblings or the rest of the family. One common characteristic of the middle child is that she is a good mediator or negotiator. She comes naturally into this role because she's often right in the middle, between big brother and little sister, whatever the case may be. And because she can't have Mom or Dad all to herself, she learns the fine art of compromise. Obviously, these skills are assets in adult life, and middle children often become the best adjusted adults in the family.

1 List some of the personality traits and behaviors that Dr. Leman attributes to middle children.

_____

_____

_____

_____

2 How might these traits and behaviors affect the middle child's relationship with his/her siblings during childhood?

_____

_____

_____

3 How might these traits and behaviors affect the middle child's relationship with his/her siblings later on in life?

_____

_____

_____

Topics for Discussion and Writing

1 Write a composition about one of your siblings. What was your relationship like? Why did you feel this way about each other? How is your relationship today? If you are an only child, write about whether you would have preferred to have siblings. Explain your preference.

2 Do you think it is important for children to have brothers and sisters? If so, how many? Do you think that only children may be at a disadvantage when they get older? Why or why not? Discuss this issue with your classmates.

3 Write a composition about the importance of the bond between siblings. How does this bond change as siblings get older? Give examples from your own life. When you need help, who do you turn to? Why? What is your birth order? Do you think your role in your family has been influenced by your position? If so, in what ways?

4 **Write in your journal.** Which member of your family assumes the kin-keeping role described in this article? Why?

Follow-up Activities

1 Refer to the **Self-Evaluation of Reading Strategies** on the next page. Think about the strategies you used to understand "Beyond Rivalry." Check off the strategies you used. Evaluate your strategy use over the first three chapters. Which strategies have you begun to use that you didn't use in the first or second chapter? Which strategies do you use consistently? Which additional strategies do you use that you have added to the list? To what extent have you applied these strategies to other reading you do?

Self-Evaluation of Reading Strategies			
Strategies	Readings		
	"Hop Skip … and Software"	"My Husband, the Outsider"	"Beyond Rivalry"
I read the title and try to predict what the reading will be about.			
I use my knowledge of the world to help me understand the text.			
I read as though I *expect* the text to have meaning.			
I use illustrations to help me understand the text.			
I ask myself questions about the text.			
I use a variety of types of context clues.			
I take chances in order to identify meaning.			
I continue if I am not successful.			
I identify and underline main ideas.			
I connect details with main ideas.			
I summarize the reading in my own words.			
I skip unnecessary words.			
I look up words correctly in the dictionary.			
I connect the reading to other material I have read.			
I do not translate into my native language.			

2 Alone, or in pairs, survey several people outside class using the chart below. Interview people with at least one sibling. When you return to class, compile your data. What are the similarities and differences between your responses as a class and your interviewees' responses?

The purpose of this questionnaire is to collect data regarding people and their siblings. Interview people with at least one sibling.

Sibling Survey				
	#1	#2	#3	#4
Interviewee's gender	M / F	M / F	M / F	M / F
Questions				
1. How many brothers and sisters do you have?				
2. Where are you in terms of birth order (oldest, middle child, youngest)?				
3. As a child, how well did you get along with your siblings? very well OK not very well badly				
4. Which sibling did you get along with the best?				
5. How do you get along with your siblings today? very well OK not very well badly				
6. Of the following pairs of siblings, which pair do you think is usually the closest? a. A brother and a sister b. Two sisters c. Two brothers				
7. Which person in your family usually takes responsibility for getting family members together?				

Cloze Quiz

Complete the passage with words from the list. Use each word only once.

close	example	marriages	retirement
divorce	generation	neighbors	rift
drift	hostile	old age	sibling
estrangement	last	parent	spouses
events	link	relationships	worse

During childhood, sisters and brothers are a major part of each

other's lives, for better or for _____ . As adults they may
(1)

_____ apart as they become involved in their own careers,
(2)

marriages and families. But in later life, with _____ ,
(3)

an empty nest, and parents and sometimes _____ gone,
(4)

brothers and sisters often turn back to each other for a special affinity and

_____ to the past.
(5)

"In the stressful, fast-paced world we live in, the _____
(6)

relationship becomes for many the only intimate connection that seems to

_____ ," says psychologist Michael Kahn of the University
(7)

of Hartford. Friends and _____ may move away, former
(8)

coworkers are forgotten, _____ break up, but no matter what,
(9)

our sisters and brothers remain our sisters and brothers.

This late-life bond may be especially important to the "Baby Boom"

_____ now in adulthood, who average about two or three
(10)

siblings apiece. High _____ rates and the decision by many
(11)

couples to have only one or no children will force members of this generation

to look to their brothers and sisters for support in _____ .
(12)

Critical _____ can bring siblings together or deepen
           (13)

an existing _____ . Parental sickness or death is a prime
              (14)

_____ . Ross and Milgram found that siblings immersed in
      (15)

rivalry and conflict were even more torn apart by the death or sickness of a

_____ . Those siblings who had been _____ since
      (16)   (17)

childhood became closer.

In a study of older people with sisters and brothers, Gold found that

about 20 percent said they were either _____ or indifferent
                                            (18)

toward their siblings. Reasons for the rifts ranged from inheritance

disputes to animosity between spouses. But many of those who had poor

_____ felt guilt and remorse. A man who hadn't spoken with
      (19)

his sister in 20 years described their _____ as a "festering sore."
                                          (20)

Crossword Puzzle

Read the clues on the next page. Write the answers in the correct spaces in the puzzle.

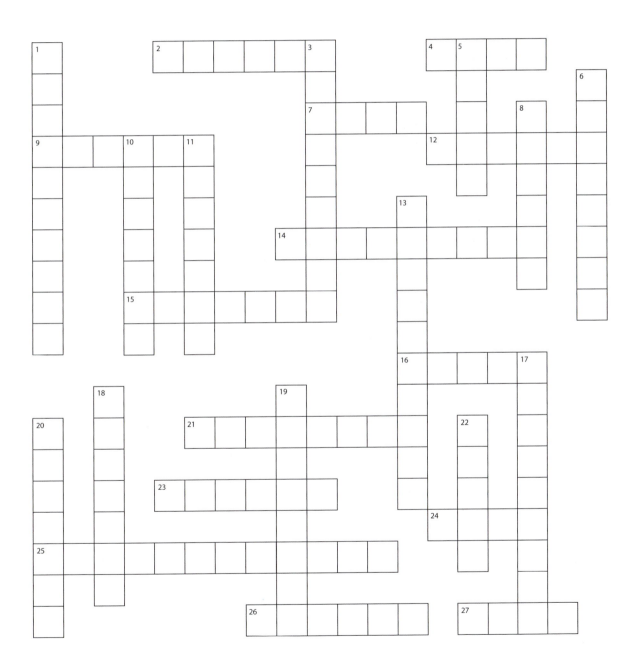

Crossword Puzzle Clues

2. We offer _____ to someone when we try to comfort him.
4. A break
7. A suit or action in law
9. When I have _____ to the Internet, I can go online whenever I wish.
12. When we _____ with others, we take opposite sides on an issue.
14. Able to speak two languages
15. Apprehension or worry
16. Bring to mind; call forth a memory
21. Confirm; verify
23. Unusual; excitingly different
24. Endure; remain unimpaired
25. Unable to get along with because of differences
26. Option
27. A tie; a uniting force

1. Estrangement
3. An _____ is something that is different from the norm.
5. Read between the lines
6. Range
8. Clan
10. Take up readily or gladly
11. Brother or sister
13. Promise or commitment to marry
17. Children go to school to get an _____.
18. Improve
19. Dwindle; decrease
20. Marriage ceremony
22. My _____ job is a dream job.

Influences on Our Lives: Nature versus Nurture

4 CHAPTER

Who Lives Longer?

Prereading Preparation

1 In groups of three or four, speculate on how long the average person lives. Discuss factors that affect a person's longevity, both positively and negatively. For example, diet is a factor. How can diet positively affect your longevity? How can it negatively affect your longevity? Use the chart below to help you organize your ideas.

Factors	Positive	Negative
diet		

2 After you have organized the factors, prepare a brief (two- or three-minute) report that one of you will present to the class.

3 After all the groups have presented their views, work in your group again. Revise your chart as needed and then report any changes to the class.

4 Read the title. Who do you think the article will say lives longer?

CD 1
Track 07

Who Lives Longer?

by Patricia Skalka, *McCall's*

1   How to live longer is a topic that has fascinated mankind for centuries. Today, scientists are beginning to separate the facts from the fallacies surrounding the aging process. Why is it that some people reach a ripe old age and others do not? Several factors influencing longevity are set at birth, but surprisingly, many
5   others are elements that can be changed. Here is what you should know.
        Some researchers divide the elements determining who will live longer into two categories: fixed factors and changeable factors. Gender, race and heredity are fixed factors—they can't be reversed, although certain long-term social changes can influence them. For example, women live longer than men—at
10   birth, their life expectancy is about seven to eight years more. However, cigarette smoking, drinking and reckless driving could shorten this advantage.
        There is increasing evidence that length of life is also influenced by a number of elements that are within your ability to control. The most obvious are physical lifestyle factors.

Health Measures

15   According to a landmark study of nearly 7,000 adults in Alameda County, California, women can add up to seven years to their lives and men 11 to 12 years by following seven simple health practices: (1) Don't smoke. (2) If you drink, do so only moderately. (3) Eat breakfast regularly. (4) Don't eat between meals. (5) Maintain normal weight. (6) Sleep about eight hours a night. (7) Exercise
20   moderately.

Cutting calories may be the single most significant lifestyle change you can make. Experiments have shown that in laboratory animals, a 40 percent calorie reduction leads to a 50 percent extension in longevity. "Eating less has a more profound and diversified effect on the aging process than does any other life-style change," says Byung P. Yu, Ph.D., professor of physiology at the University of Texas Health Science Center at San Antonio. "It is the only factor we know of in laboratory animals that is an anti-aging factor."

Psychosocial Factors

A long life, however, is not just the result of being good to your body and staving off disease. All the various factors that constitute and influence daily life can be critical too. In searching for the ingredients to a long, healthy existence, scientists are studying links between longevity and the psychological and social aspects of human existence. The following can play significant roles in determining your longevity:

Social Integration

Researchers have found that people who are socially integrated—they are part of a family network, are married, participate in structured group activities—live longer.

Early studies indicated that the more friends and relatives you had, the longer you lived. Newer studies focus on the types of relationships that are most beneficial. "Larger networks don't always seem to be advantageous to women," says epidemiologist Teresa Seeman, Ph.D., associate research scientist at Yale University. "Certain kinds of ties add more demands rather than generate more help."

Autonomy

A feeling of autonomy or control can come from having a say in important decisions (where you live, how you spend your money) or from being surrounded by people who inspire confidence in your ability to master certain tasks (yes, you can quit smoking, you will get well). Studies show these feelings bring a sense of well-being and satisfaction with life. "Autonomy is a key factor in successful aging," says Toni Antonucci, associate research scientist at the Institute for Social Research at the University of Michigan.

Stress and Job Satisfaction

50   Researchers disagree on how these factors affect longevity. There isn't enough data available to support a link between stress and longevity, says Edward L. Schneider, M.D., dean of the Andrus Gerontology Center at the University of Southern California. Animal research, however, provides exciting insights. In studies with laboratory rats, certain types of stress damage the immune system

55 and destroy brain cells, especially those involved in memory. Other kinds of stress enhance immune function by 20 to 30 percent, supporting a theory first advanced by Hans Selye, M.D., Ph.D., a pioneer in stress research. He proposed that an exciting, active and meaningful life contributes to good health.

    The relationship between job satisfaction and longevity also remains in

60 question. According to some researchers, a satisfying job adds years to a man's life, while volunteer work increases a woman's longevity. These findings may change as more women participate in the workforce. One study found that clerical workers suffered twice as many heart attacks as homemakers. Factors associated with the coronary problems were suppressed hostility, having a

65 nonsupportive boss, and decreased job mobility.

Environment

    Where you live can make a difference in how long you live. A study by the California Department of Health Services in Berkeley found a 40 percent higher mortality rate among people living in a poverty area compared to those in a nonpoverty area. "The difference was not due to age, sex, health

70 care or lifestyle," says George A. Kaplan, Ph.D., chief of the department's Human Population Laboratory. The resulting hypothesis: A locale can have environmental characteristics, such as polluted air or water, or socioeconomic characteristics, such as a high crime rate and level of stress, that make it unhealthy.

Socioeconomic Status

75   People with higher incomes, more education and high-status occupations tend to live longer. Researchers used to think this was due to better living and job conditions, nutrition and access to health care, but these theories have not held up. Nevertheless, the differences can be dramatic. Among women 65 to 74 years old, those with less than an eighth-grade education are much more

80 likely to die than are women who have completed at least one year of college.

What Can You Do?

The message from the experts is clear. There are many ways to add years to your life. Instituting sound health practices and expanding your circle of acquaintances and activities will have a beneficial effect. The good news about aging, observes Erdman B. Palmore of the Center for the Study of Aging and Human Development at Duke Medical Center in North Carolina, is many of the factors related to longevity are also related to life satisfaction.

85

Reading Overview: Main Idea, Details, and Summary

Read the passage again. As you read, underline what you think are the most important ideas. Then, in one or two sentences, write the main idea of the reading. **Use your own words.**

Main Idea

_____

_____

_____

Details

Complete the chart below to organize the information in the article. Refer back to the information you underlined in the passage as a guide. When you have finished, write a brief summary of the reading. **Use your own words.**

Who Lives Longer?		
_____	Changeable Factors	
	_____	_____
1. gender	1.	1.
2.	2.	2.
3.	3.	3.
	4.	4.
	5.	5.
	6.	
	7.	

What you can do:

1. _____

_____

2. _____

_____

Summary

_____

_____

_____

_____

_____

Statement Evaluation

Read the statements. Then scan the article to find out if each sentence is **True (T)**, **False (F)**, or **Not Mentioned (NM)** in the article. Write **T, F,** or **NM.**

1 _____ There is nothing you can do to increase longevity.

2 _____ Laboratory rats that exercised lived longer than those that did not exercise.

3 _____ Eating less may help you live longer.

4 _____ There may be a connection between longevity and psychological factors.

5 _____ Women who work outside the home have more heart attacks than working men do.

6 _____ People who live in poverty areas live longer than people who live in nonpoverty areas.

7 _____ People with higher socioeconomic status tend to live longer than those with lower socioeconomic status.

C

Reading Analysis

Read each question carefully. Either circle the letter or number of the correct answer or write your answer in the space provided.

1 Read lines 1–3.

  a. Which word means the opposite of **fact?**

  _____

  b. How do you know?

  _____

2 Read lines 3–4. People who **reach a ripe old age** are people who

  a. die young

  b. are women

  c. live a long time

3 Read lines 6–9. **Fixed factors** are those that

    a. we can change
    b. we are born with
    c. can be reversed

4 In lines 8–9, and 34–35, what follows the **dashes (—)**?

    a. Explanations
    b. Causes
    c. New ideas

5 Read lines 7–11. What are examples of **certain long-term social changes?**

_____

6 Read lines 17–18. **If you drink, do so only moderately.** What does this sentence about alcohol mean?

    a. Do not drink.
    b. Drink as much as you want.
    c. Only drink a little.

7 Read lines 32–33. What does **the following** refer to?

_____

8 Read lines 43–46. **Having a say** means

    a. having an opinion
    b. having a choice
    c. speaking loudly

9 Read line 50. What do **these factors** refer to?

_____

10 Read lines 62–65. **The coronary problems** are

    a. hostility
    b. dissatisfaction with your job
    c. heart attacks

11 Read lines 69–74. What is a **hypothesis?**

    a. A theory
    b. A fact
    c. A law

Dictionary Skills

Read the excerpts from the article. Then read the dictionary entry for the boldfaced word and write the number of the definition that is appropriate for the context. Be prepared to explain your choice.

1 The study of nearly 7,000 adults in California was a **landmark** in the field of health. According to the study, women can add up to seven years to their lives and men 11 to 12 years by following seven simple health practices.

landmark: _____

> **landmark** **1** : an object (as a stone or tree) that marks the boundary of land **2 a** : a conspicuous object on land that marks a locality **b** : an anatomical structure used as a point of orientation in locating other structures **3** : an event or development that marks a turning point or a stage **4** : a structure (as a building) of unusual historical and usually aesthetic interest; *especially* : one that is officially designated and set aside for preservation

2 Eating less has a more **profound** effect on the aging process than does any other lifestyle change. It is the only factor we know of in laboratory animals that is an anti-aging factor.

profound: _____

> **profound** **1 a** : having intellectual depth and insight **b** : difficult to fathom or understand **2 a** : extending far below the surface **b** : coming from, reaching to, or situated at a depth : DEEP-SEATED <a profound sigh> **3 a** : characterized by intensity of feeling or quality **b** : all encompassing : COMPLETE <profound sleep> <profound deafness>…

3 A feeling of autonomy or control can come from having a **say** in important decisions (where you live, how you spend your money).

say: _____

> **say** **1** *archaic* : something that is said : STATEMENT **2** : an expression of opinion <had my say> **3** : a right or power to influence action or decision; *especially* : the authority to make final decisions

4 Instituting **sound** health practices and expanding your circle of acquaintances and activities will have a beneficial effect.

sound: _____

> **sound** **1** **a** : free from injury or disease **b** : free from flaw, defect, or decay **2** : SOLID, FIRM; *also* : STABLE **3** **a** : free from error, fallacy, or misapprehension <sound reasoning> **b** : exhibiting or based on thorough knowledge and experience <sound scholarship> **c** : legally valid <a sound title> **d** : logically valid and having true premises **e** : agreeing with accepted views : ORTHODOX **4** **a** : THOROUGH **b** : deep and undisturbed <a sound sleep> **c** : HARD, SEVERE <a sound whipping> **5** : showing good judgment or sense <sound advice> …

Thesaurus	*sound* Also look up:
adj.	safe, sturdy, undamaged, whole, logical, valid, wise; *(ant.)* illogical, unreliable

E

Critical Thinking Strategies

Read each question carefully, and write a response. Remember that there is no one correct answer. Your response depends on what **you** think.

1 What tone does the author set at the end of the article? Is she upbeat, pessimistic, matter-of-fact, etc.?

_____

_____

2 Does the author of "Who Lives Longer?" believe that increasing life expectancy is a desirable goal? Explain your answer.

_____

_____

_____

3 Why does eating have such a dramatic positive effect on longevity?

_____

_____

4 Why do you think volunteer work increases a woman's longevity?

_____

_____

_____

5 How are clerical workers and homemakers similar? Why do you think clerical workers suffer twice as many heart attacks as homemakers?

_____

_____

_____

UNIT 2   INFLUENCES ON OUR LIVES: NATURE VERSUS NURTURE

Another Perspective

Read the article and answer the questions that follow.

CD 1
Track 08

More Senior Citizens, Fewer Kids

by Jessie Cheng, *Free China Review*

1   "Thirty years from now, it will be rare to see children walking along the streets of Taiwan," says Chen Kuanjeng, a research fellow in the Institute of Sociology at Academia Sinica. "Instead, the streets will be full of elderly people." Chen's prediction may sound a bit drastic, but he voices a growing concern among sociologists over the dramatic shift under way in Taiwan society toward
5   a graying population. As in many developed countries, island families are having fewer children, while at the same time the average life span is increasing to create a larger and larger pool of senior citizens.

Between 1953 and 1993, the annual birthrate declined from about forty-five
10   births per thousand persons to less than sixteen. During the same period, the average number of children per Taiwan couple declined by more than two-thirds, from 7 to 1.7. The current average is below that of the United States (2 children per couple), mainland China (1.9), and Britain or France (both 1.8). The Taiwan figure also means that since 1984 the birthrate has dropped below
15   the "replacement level." Sociologists predict that within forty years, the total population will be declining.

Another trend is also changing the face of Taiwan's population: the average life span is steadily rising, leading to a growing proportion of elderly people. In 1951, local men lived an average of 53 years, and women lived 56 years. Today,
20   men average 72 years and women 77. Because the trend toward fewer children and more senior citizens is expected to continue, sociologists predict that the elderly proportion of the population will increase steadily. While persons aged over 65 made up just over seven percent of the population in 1994, they are expected to account for 22 percent by the year 2036—a figure that could mean
25   more than five million senior citizens.

The result is an overall "graying" of society and a new set of social welfare needs that must be met—nursing homes rather than nursery schools, day care programs for the elderly rather than for preschoolers. Social scientists predict these demands will be hard to fulfill. "In the future, there won't be
30   enough young people to support the older people," says Chen. Sociologists are particularly concerned that expanding health care costs for senior citizens will

mean a large financial burden for taxpayers. Another concern is that a dwindling population of working-age adults will slow economic growth.

Patterns in Taiwan's population growth looked far different just a generation ago. During the 1950s, the island's population zoomed from 7.6 million to a 1960 figure of 10.8 million. The centuries-old belief that more children bring luck to a family was strong among local residents.

But as the decade came to a close, the rapid population increase began to alarm sociologists. Opposition notwithstanding, the government launched a pre-pregnancy health campaign in 1959 which included teaching birth control methods through public hospitals and health stations (community out-patient clinics). Still, Taiwan's population grew from 14.7 million to 17.8 million during the 1970s, and social scientists continued to urge further population control measures.

The 1980s marked a turning point in population control. In addition to official family planning campaigns, a number of social factors have led to the declining birthrate. For example, couples are marrying later, and a growing number of young people are opting to stay single.

But sociologists worry that population control measures have gone too far. The government is now reversing its official stance on family planning. "While in past decades we controlled the population, over the next few years we will promote a reasonable growth rate," says Chien Tai-lang, director of the Department of Population, Ministry of the Interior.

1. Which two important population factors in Taiwan does this article discuss?

_____

_____

2. How are these factors expected to affect Taiwan in the future?

_____

_____

3. What potential problems might this population shift create?

_____

_____

4. Why is the birthrate declining?

_____

_____

UNIT 2   INFLUENCES ON OUR LIVES: NATURE VERSUS NURTURE

G Topics for Discussion and Writing

1. What are some of the consequences of an aging population? In other words, what factors must be taken into consideration as the elderly begin to make up a larger segment of a country's population than ever before? What needs will have to be met?

2. In a small group, discuss the factors that might shorten a person's life expectancy.

3. In a small group, make a list of the steps you can take to increase your life expectancy.

4. Refer to the "Global Life Expectancy at Birth" map on page 79. Choose a country from the map. Write a composition about the life expectancy in this country. Include what you think may be reasons for this country's high or low life expectancy.

5. **Write in your journal.** How long would you like to live? Explain your answer.

H Follow-up Activities

1. Refer to the **Self-Evaluation of Reading Strategies** on page 114. Think about the strategies you used to understand "Who Lives Longer?" Check off the strategies you used. Think about the strategies you didn't use, and apply them to understand the readings that follow.

2 Study the chart; then answer the questions that follow.

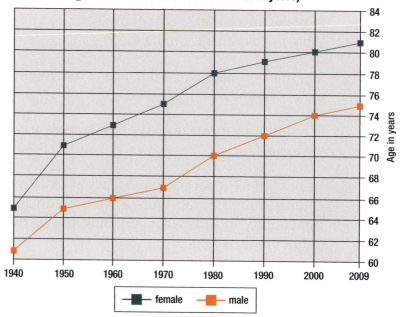

Life Expectancy in the United States
(years indicated are individuals' birth years)

a. What does this chart illustrate?

_____

b. 1. About how long can a female born in 2000 expect to live?

_____

   2. About how long can a male born in 2000 expect to live?

_____

c. In what decades was there the greatest difference in life expectancy for males and females?

_____

d. In what decade did life expectancy for females make the greatest gain? How many years did females gain?

_____

e. In what decade did life expectancy for males make the greatest gain? How many years did males gain?

_____

f. In general terms, speculate on what could account for this great increase in life expectancy for *both* sexes in the particular decade?

_____

_____

3 Study the map; then answer the questions that follow.

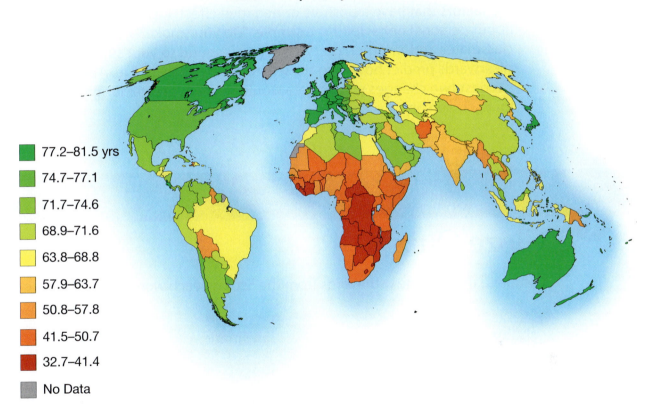

Global Life Expectancy at Birth in 2009

77.2–81.5 yrs
74.7–77.1
71.7–74.6
68.9–71.6
63.8–68.8
57.9–63.7
50.8–57.8
41.5–50.7
32.7–41.4
No Data

a. What does this map illustrate?

_____

b. Locate your country on the map. What is the average life expectancy?

_____

c. What is the highest life expectancy in the world? Where is it?

_____

d. What is the lowest life expectancy in the world? Where is it?

_____

CHAPTER 4   WHO LIVES LONGER?

e. What are some factors that might account for such a range in life expectancy throughout the world, e.g., from 32.7 to 81.5?

_____

_____

4 Work with a partner. Plan a healthy diet for yourselves. Compare your diet with your classmates' diets. As a class, decide which diet is the healthiest.

5 Work with a partner to design a survey to predict life expectancy, using the factors that have a positive or negative effect. Include questions about personal behavior (for example, "Do you smoke?"). Ask your classmates and/or other interviewees to respond to your survey. Afterwards predict how long these people are likely to live. Also, suggest two changes you believe would result in greater longevity for each person.

I Cloze Quiz

Complete the passage with words from the list. Use each word only once.

ability	expectancy	landmark	reversed
birth	fallacies	longer	ripe
changeable	health	longevity	separate
elements	heredity	maintain	shorten
evidence	influence	moderately	years

How to live _____(1)_____ is a topic that has fascinated mankind for centuries. Today, scientists are beginning to _____(2)_____ the facts from the _____(3)_____ surrounding the aging process. Why is it that some people reach a _____(4)_____ old age and others do not? Several factors influencing _____ (5) are set at _____ (6) , but surprisingly, many others are elements that can be changed. Here is what you should know.

Some researchers divide the _____ (7) determining who will live longer into two categories: fixed factors and _____ (8) factors. Gender, race and _____ (9) are fixed factors—they can't be _____ (10) , although certain long-term social changes can _____ (11) them. For example, women live longer than men—at birth, their life _____ (12) is about seven to eight years more. However, cigarette smoking, drinking and reckless driving could _____ (13) this advantage.

There is increasing _____ (14) that length of life is also influenced by a number of elements that are within your _____ (15) to control. The most obvious are physical lifestyle factors.

According to a _____ (16) study of nearly 7,000 adults in Alameda County, California, women can add up to seven _____ (17) to their lives and men 11 to 12 years by following seven simple _____ (18) practices: Don't smoke. If you drink, do so only _____ (19) . Eat breakfast regularly. Don't eat between meals. _____ (20) normal weight. Sleep about eight hours a night. Exercise moderately.

5 CHAPTER

Switched at Birth: Women Learn the Truth 56 Years Later

Prereading Preparation

1. Look at the photo and read the title of the article.

   a. What does **switched at birth** mean?

   _____

   _____

   b. What do you think happened to these two women?

   _____

   _____

   c. What is **the truth?**

   _____

   d. When did they learn **the truth?**

   _____

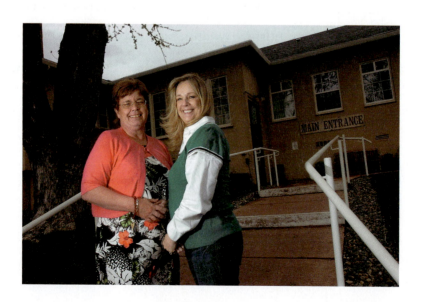

Switched at Birth: Women Learn the Truth 56 Years Later

by Imaeyen Ibanga, *ABC News*

1   When Oregon nurses handed Marjorie Angell her newborn daughter in the hospital in 1953, she insisted they had given her the wrong child. Her concerns were brushed off, but in an unlikely story that was 56 years in the making, her mother's intuition foreshadowed what was to come.

5   It was true. Her daughter had been switched at birth when she and the other baby were being bathed, but Marjorie Angell would never learn the truth because she died before it was revealed. "It's sad," DeeAnn Angell Schafer told "Good Morning America." "Just to think I missed out on knowing my own parents." Even though Kay Rene Reed Qualls said she enjoyed a wonderful life, she still feels guilty about 10 the memories that should belong to DeeAnn and her family. "I look at them and I feel like I cheated somebody," she said. The story of two women who grew up in the wrong families just came to light last month to the surprise of everyone and no one.

A Secret Switch?

On May 3, 1953, DeeAnn Angell of Fossil, Oregon, and Kay Rene Reed of Condon, Oregon, were born at Pioneer Memorial Hospital in the eastern Oregon town of Heppner. They grew up, got married, and had children and 15 grandchildren of their own. The women's lives were uneventful until last summer, when Kay Rene's brother, Bobby Reed, received a call from an 86-year-old woman who claimed to hold an astonishing secret. He met the woman in her nursing home. She said she had known the Reeds' mother and had lived next door to the Angell family in Fossil. Her shocking claim was that Kay Rene 20 wasn't really a Reed at all; she was an Angell. The elderly woman said Kay Rene and DeeAnn were switched at birth. To bolster her story, she showed Bobby Reed an old photo of DeeAnn's sister. Reed saw an instant and undeniable resemblance to the woman raised as his sister.

Switched at Birth: Uncovering the Truth

If what the elderly woman said was correct, then DeeAnn really was Reed's 25 sister and not Kay Rene. The secret stunned Reed, who was unsure what to do with the potential bombshell. He always had known and loved Kay Rene as his sister. Though Kay Rene was a brunette in a sea of blonds, no one ever thought to question her paternity.

30 　Reed didn't want anything to change, nor did he want to hurt anyone. He decided to tell his two oldest sisters, and one of them broke the news to Kay Rene. With both the Reed parents and the Angell parents dead, the children had to come together to uncover the truth about the alleged mix-up.

　The families learned rumors of babies being switched at birth had been
35 around for decades. In fact, Kay Rene first learned of such gossip in 1995 when her sister Carol told her during their dying father's last camping trip. After his death, Kay Rene's mother approached her about the subject. She acknowledged that she heard another new mother in the same hospital, where she had given birth, question if her baby was her own. But after looking into Kay Rene's big
40 brown eyes, she determined this was her baby and she wouldn't bring the issue up anymore.

Growing Up with Questions

　Growing up, Kay Rene had questioned whether she truly was a Reed. She had her suspicions. She knew she didn't look like anyone else in her family. Eventually, Kay Rene said, the rumors started in her family that maybe she
45 wasn't really related to them.

　"I think all the older sisters knew this," she said. But neither woman ever had blood tests and DNA testing was not an option.

　The doubts just lingered. Even Kay Rene's husband joked about whether the Reeds truly were her relatives after seeing her at family functions. Kay Rene just
50 knew she didn't want those thoughts to be true. She chalked them up to being ornery. She justified her placement in the Reed clan by saying her blue eyes came from her father. DeeAnn, too, had suspicions growing up. She wondered why she loved horses so much. She received a phone call from her sister in February to tell her about the news—the rumors might be true.

'Swisters': Switched Sisters

55 　Kay Rene wanted to know the truth; she needed to know it. So last month, she, her brother and their sister Dorothy met the blond-haired DeeAnn at a Kennewick, Washington, clinic for a DNA test. When Kay Rene finally met the Angell family, she realized she looked more like them. The DNA test confirmed what Kay Rene had seen with her own eyes and what DeeAnn realized the
60 second she met Kay Rene. Kay Rene was not a Reed and had no biological link to her brother Bobby Reed. DeeAnn actually was Bobby Reed's sister and Kay Rene really was an Angell.

The news was shocking and disturbing for Kay Rene, who felt as if she had lived a lie. She questioned if her memories actually belonged to her since she lived what should have been DeeAnn's life. DeeAnn finally got the answer to why she had an affinity for horses. Her biological father had been a horse trainer. DeeAnn and Kay Rene have become close following the revelation. They refer to each other as swisters, short for switched sisters.

The hospital where the women were born has offered them counseling, but neither has accepted the offer. "We're old women now," Kay Rene said. They also haven't decided if they'll sue the facility. And while DeeAnn harbors at least some anger about the situation, Kay Rene said she doesn't because there's no use in it.

Reading Overview: Main Idea, Details, and Summary

Read the passage again. As you read, underline what you think are the most important ideas. Then, in one or two sentences, write the main idea of the reading. **Use your own words.**

Main Idea

_____

_____

_____

Details

Use the following chart to organize the information in the article. Refer back to the information you underlined in the passage as a guide. When you have finished, write a brief summary of the reading. **Use your own words.**

Switched at Birth: Women Learn the Truth 56 Years Later	
What happened?	
When did this happen?	
Where did this happen?	
How did this happen?	
Who was Kay Rene's biological mother?	
Who was DeeAnn's biological mother?	
How did they learn the truth?	
How does Kay Rene feel about what happened?	
How does DeeAnn feel about what happened?	

Summary

_____

_____

_____

_____

_____

B Statement Evaluation

Read the statements. Then scan the article to find out if each sentence is **True (T), False (F),** or an **Inference (I).** Write **T, F,** or **I.**

1. _____ DeeAnn and Kay Rene are sisters.

2. _____ The 86-year-old neighbor had been at the hospital when DeeAnn and Kay Rene were born.

3. _____ Bobby Reed's sister told Kay Rene the truth about being switched at birth.

4. _____ Kay Rene did not resemble the Reed family.

5. _____ Both women had suspicions about their origins.

6. _____ DeeAnn's and Kay Rene's parents knew for sure about their daughters having been switched at birth.

7. _____ DeeAnn was the only person in the Angell family who loved horses.

8. _____ DeeAnn and Kay Rene refused counseling from the hospital where they were born.

C Reading Analysis

Read each question carefully. Circle the letter or number of the correct answer, or write the answer.

1. Read lines 1–4.
   a. What were Marjorie Angell's concerns?
      1. She believed her newborn daughter was ill.
      2. She felt very ill after her daughter's birth.
      3. She believed she was given the wrong baby.
   b. **Her concerns were brushed off** means
      1. no one listened to her concerns
      2. no one helped her with her concerns
      3. no one understood her concerns

c. **Her mother's intuition foreshadowed what was to come.** This means

   1. the nurses were right, and Marjorie Angell was wrong

   2. Marjorie Angell's mother was right, and the nurses were wrong

   3. Marjorie Angell was right, and the nurses were wrong

2 In line 8, DeeAnn Angell says, **I missed out on knowing my own parents.** Why didn't DeeAnn know her parents?

   a. Her parents died before she learned about the switch.

   b. Her parents were very young when they died.

   c. She lived with the wrong family.

3 Read lines 11–12. Which word is a synonym for **came to light?**

_____

4 Read lines 16–24.

   a. Who called Bobby Reed last summer?

      1. Kay Rene

      2. An elderly neighbor of the Angell family

      3. A nurse from the nursing home

   b. What secret did she tell him?

      1. She knew both the Angell and the Reed families.

      2. She lived in a nursing home next door to the Reeds.

      3. DeeAnn and Kay Rene were switched at birth.

   c. What proof did she show Bobby Reed?

      1. A picture of DeeAnn's biological sister

      2. A picture of Bobby Reed's mother

      3. A picture of DeeAnn when she was young

5 Read lines 26–29.

   a. **The secret stunned Reed** means

      1. he was afraid

      2. he was shocked

      3. he was excited

   b. What was **the potential bombshell?**

      1. Kay Rene was not really his sister.

      2. DeeAnn was not really his sister.

      3. Kay Rene looked different from her family.

    c. **No one ever thought to question her paternity** means

       1. no one asked Kay Rene any questions
       2. no one asked about Kay Rene's real family
       3. no one wondered who Kay Rene's father was

6 Read lines 36–41.

    a. Did Kay Rene's mother know that the other mother had wondered if the babies were switched at the hospital?

       1. No   2. Yes

    b. Kay Rene's mother **wouldn't bring the issue up anymore.** This means that

       1. she decided not to ask any questions about the possibility that this wasn't her baby
       2. she decided not to meet the other new mother in the hospital that had questions about the baby
       3. she was sure that Kay Rene was her baby because she had brown eyes

7 Read lines 42–52.

    a. **Kay Rene had questioned whether she truly was a Reed.** Why?

    _____

    b. What are **suspicions?**

       1. Questions
       2. Uncertainties
       3. Ideas

    c. What is a **clan?**

       1. An inherited trait such as eye color
       2. A group of related people
       3. A special interest in something

8 Read lines 55–62.

    a. Why did the two women have DNA tests?

    _____

    b. What did the DNA tests confirm?

       1. Kay Rene was not a member of the Reed family; she was an Angell.
       2. DeeAnn was not a member of the Reed family; she was an Angell.
       3. Bobby Reed was really Kay Rene's brother.

9 Read lines 71–73.

    a. Who is angry about the switch?

        1. Kay Rene
        2. DeeAnn
        3. Both DeeAnn and Kay Rene

    b. One of the women isn't angry **because there's no use in it.** This means

        1. she doesn't care about the switch because she had a good life
        2. she doesn't want to sue the hospital because she's old now
        3. she doesn't feel anger because it's useless to be angry

D Dictionary Skills

Read the excerpts from the article. Then read the dictionary entry for the boldfaced word and write the number of the definition that is appropriate for the context. Be prepared to explain your choice.

1 Her shocking **claim** was that Kay Rene wasn't really a Reed at all; she was an Angell.

claim: _____

> **claim** **1** : a demand for something due or believed to be due <an insurance claim> **2** **a** : a right to something; *specifically* : a title to a debt, privilege, or other thing in the possession of another **b** : an assertion open to challenge <a claim of authenticity> **3** : something that is claimed; *especially* : a tract of land staked out

2 The doubts just **lingered.**

linger: _____

> **linger** *intransitive verb* **1** : to be slow in parting or in quitting something : TARRY <fans linger*ed* outside the door> **2** **a** : to remain alive although gradually dying **b** : to remain existent although often waning in strength, importance, or influence <linger*ing* doubts> <linger*ing* odors> . . . **4** : to move slowly . . .

By permission. From *Merriam-Webster's Collegiate® Dictionary*, 11th Edition © 2010 by Merriam-Webster, Incorporated (www.Merriam-Webster.com).

3 Even Kay Rene's husband joked about whether the Reeds truly were her relatives after seeing her at family **functions.**

function: _____

> **function** **1** : professional or official position : OCCUPATION **2** : the action for which a person or thing is specially fitted or used or for which a thing exists : PURPOSE **3** : any of a group of related actions contributing to a larger action; *especially* : the normal and specific contribution of a bodily part to the economy of a living organism **4** : an official or formal ceremony or social gathering . . .

4 And while DeeAnn **harbors** at least some anger about the situation, Kay Rene said she doesn't because there's no use in it.

harbor: _____

> **harbor** **1** **a** : to give shelter or refuge to **b** : to be the home or habitat of <the ledges still harbor rattlesnakes>; *broadly* : CONTAIN **2** : to hold especially persistently in the mind : CHERISH <harbor*ed* a grudge> . . .

Thesaurus	*function* Also look up:
n.	action, duty, job, responsibility, celebration, gathering, occasion
v.	operate, perform, work

By permission. From *Merriam-Webster's Collegiate® Dictionary*, 11th Edition © 2010 by Merriam-Webster, Incorporated (www.Merriam-Webster.com).

Critical Thinking Strategies

Read each question carefully, and write a response. Remember that there is no one correct answer. Your response depends on what **you** think.

1 Marjorie Angell insisted the nurses had given her the wrong child, but no one believed her. Why do you think the nurses didn't believe Marjorie Angell?

_____

_____

_____

2 Kay Rene Reed Qualls said she enjoyed a wonderful life, but she still feels guilty. Why do you think she feels this way?

_____

_____

_____

3 Bobby Reed received a call from an 86-year-old woman who said that Kay Rene wasn't really a Reed at all; she was an Angell. Why do you think she waited such a long time to tell the truth?

_____

_____

_____

Another Perspective

Read the article and answer the questions that follow.

CD 1
Track 10

Polish Twins Swapped by Doctors as Babies Receive Damages

by Michael Leidig, *Telegraph Media Group*

1   A court in Poland has awarded almost £350,000 (US $584,600) in damages to the families of two girls who were mistakenly swapped by hospital staff when they were babies. The ruling in Warsaw brings to a close a seven-year battle for the families after their daughters discovered their true identities.

5   Kasia and Nina Ofmanska, who are identical twins, were taken to a Warsaw hospital after developing pneumonia in 1984, when they were two weeks old. While they were there, staff mistakenly switched Nina with another girl, Edyta Wierzbicka. Neither set of parents noticed and, as the "twins" grew up, doctors explained their startling differences by claiming that they had never been identical.

10 The separated twins grew up just a few miles from each other in Warsaw and were only reunited when an old school friend of one of the girls said she had another friend who was the spitting image of her. Kasia and Nina—now aged 25—came face to face and the shocking truth began to unravel. "Oh God, she was just like me. We even walk the same way," said Kasia. Nina added: "We were
15 seeing each other for the first time, but I felt as if I knew everything about her."

    Now their parents are trying to piece their family back together after the court ruling ended their struggle to force Poland's medical authorities to admit their error. Both sets of parents have received counseling. The twins were born prematurely to their mother, Elzbieta Ofmanska, in one hospital while Edyta's
20 mother, Halina Wierzbicka, gave birth at a nearby clinic on December 15, 1983. But all three premature babies developed lung infections and were transferred separately to a third hospital, the Saskiej Kepie Clinic, at which Nina and Edyta were mixed up.

    Warning bells started to sound almost immediately when Nina's real mother
25 was told by doctors that a slight foot deformity she had been born with had miraculously cured itself. "People always ask us how on earth it was possible that we didn't notice that Nina wasn't Nina," Mrs. Ofmanska said. "But you have to understand that she went into an incubator as soon as she was born. As they grew up, the Ofmanska "twins" grew more and more different.

30   "Nina—or the girl we thought was Nina—was very shy, calm and law-abiding. But Kasia was more boisterous and more emotionally extrovert. She never played with dolls but liked to get out of the house, to ski and sail." It was only when the friend introduced the separated twins, aged 17, that the truth finally dawned. They had got the same exam grades at school and had
35 boyfriends with the same name.

    The real Nina then met her birth parents and the two families realized what had happened in the hospital. While the twins were delighted at their reunion, the parents were devastated and angry. Mrs. Ofmanska said of her rediscovered daughter: "I gave birth to her, but after that I missed the whole of my daughter's
40 childhood and can never get it back. It's hard to believe that she was here in our home, as a tiny baby, for just nine days after she came home from hospital. But after that we lost her, we weren't there for her for 17 years."

Kasia Ofmanska, who was mistakenly separated at birth from her twin sister, poses in Warsaw with a picture of her biological sister, Nina Ofmanska (right) and a picture of Edyta Wierzbicka (left), whom she and her parents thought for years was her twin.

1 For how long was this switched-baby case in the courts before it was settled?

_____

2 Why might the parents not have noticed that the daughter they took to the hospital had been switched for another baby?

_____

_____

3 When did the girls discover they had an identical twin? Who made them suspicious of this fact?

_____

_____

4 Why did the parents have to take the medical authorities to court?

_____

_____

5 How were the babies mixed up? What were the circumstances of the mix-up?

_____

_____

6 What made Mrs. Ofmanska suspicious that Nina might not be Nina?

_____

7 Why didn't Mrs. Ofmanska notice that her baby wasn't Nina?

_____

8 How were "Nina" and Kasia different?

_____

_____

9 When the error was finally revealed, how did the family members react to the news?

_____

G

Topics for Discussion and Writing

1. The Polish court awarded almost £350,000 (US $584,600) in damages to the families of two girls who were mistakenly swapped by hospital staff when they were babies. Do you agree with the court's decision? Explain your answer.

2. Although Kay Rene Reed is not angry at the hospital that made the mistake when she and DeeAnn Angell were born, DeeAnn still harbors anger. Which woman do you agree with? In other words, would you be angry in this situation? Why or why not?

3. What do you think Kay Rene and DeeAnn will do in the future, now that they know the truth? Will they become close to their biological families? Will they become close to each other? Will they decide to sue the hospital?

4. **Write in your journal.** You are a parent, and have raised your child from birth, believing that he or she was really yours. One day you discover that your child, who is now an adult, is not your biological son or daughter, but was switched at birth. How would you feel? What would you do?

H

Follow-up Activities

1. Refer to the **Self-Evaluation of Reading Strategies** on page 114. Think about the strategies you used to understand "Switched at Birth: Women Learn the Truth 56 Years Later." Check off the strategies you used. Think about the strategies you didn't use, and apply them to help you understand the readings that follow.

2. Work with a partner. You are employed by a local hospital to develop procedures to ensure that babies are never given to the wrong mother. Create a list of guidelines that must be followed by the doctors and nurses at your hospital. Compare your guidelines as a class. Draft a set of regulations for hospital personnel to follow.

I

Cloze Quiz

Complete the passage with words from the list. Use each word only once.

bathed	elderly	lived	shocking
birth	everyone	married	story
born	foreshadowed	nursing	switched
concerns	insisted	revealed	true
daughter	light	secret	uneventful

When Oregon nurses handed Marjorie Angell her newborn

_____ in the hospital in 1953, she _____ they
    (1)   (2)

had given her the wrong child. Her _____ were brushed off,
                                        (3)

but in an unlikely _____ that was 56 years in the making, her
                        (4)

mother's intuition _____ what was to come.
                        (5)

It was _____ . Her daughter had been switched
            (6)

at _____ when she and the other baby were being
        (7)

_____ , but Marjorie Angell would never learn the truth
        (8)

because she died before it was _____ . The story of two women
                                    (9)

who grew up in the wrong families just came to _____ last
                                                    (10)

month to the surprise of _____ and no one.
                            (11)

On May 3, 1953, DeeAnn Angell of Fossil, Oregon, and Kay Rene Reed of

Condon, Oregon, were _____ at Pioneer Memorial Hospital in
                        (12)

the eastern Oregon town of Heppner. They grew up, got _____ ,
                                                            (13)

and had children and grandchildren of their own. The women's lives

were _____ until last summer, when Kay Rene's brother,
        (14)

Bobby Reed, received a call from an 86-year-old woman who claimed

to hold an astonishing _____ . He met the woman in her
                                (15)

_____ home. She said she had known the Reeds' mother
        (16)

and had _____ next door to the Angell family in Fossil. Her
               (17)

_____ claim was that Kay Rene wasn't really a Reed at all; she
        (18)

was an Angell. The _____ woman said Kay Rene and DeeAnn
                              (19)

were _____ at birth.
            (20)

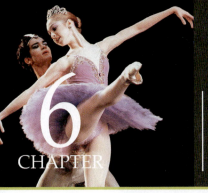

6
CHAPTER

Are Gifted Children Born or Made?

Prereading Preparation

1 Read the passages about two child prodigies.

Passage One

Wolfgang Amadeus Mozart (1756–1791)

Mozart (born in Salzburg, Austria) is widely considered to be one of the world's greatest child prodigies in music because of the amazing musical feats that he mastered at an early age. It is unclear whether he had a photographic memory or simply was trained so extensively that he was able to become highly skilled at music at such an early age, but whatever the case may be, he certainly excelled in this area. Born in 1756, Mozart began playing the harpsichord at age three and could read and play music by age five. He made his debut on the classical music scene one year later and went on to be one of the most prolific composers of all time.

Passage Two

This Korean super-genius was born in 1962 and might be the smartest guy alive today. By the age of four he was already able to read in Japanese, Korean, German, and English. On his fifth birthday, he solved complicated differential and integral calculus problems. Later, on Japanese television, he demonstrated his proficiency in Chinese, Spanish, Vietnamese, Tagalog, German, English, Japanese, and Korean. Kim was listed in the *Guinness Book of World Records* under "Highest IQ"; the book estimated the boy's score at over 210.

Kim was a guest student of physics at Hanyang University from the age of three to six. At the age of seven, he was invited to America by NASA. He finished his university studies, eventually getting a Ph.D. in physics at Colorado State University before he was 15. In 1974, during his university studies, he began research work at NASA and continued this work until his return to Korea in 1978, where he decided to switch from physics to civil engineering and eventually received a doctorate in that field. Kim was offered the chance to study at the most prestigious universities in Korea, but instead chose to attend a provincial university. Today, he serves as adjunct faculty at Chungbuk National University.

2 Work in small groups to complete the chart below.

Questions	Mozart	Kim
Why was this person such an unusual child?		
What was this person's special talent as a child?		
What were this person's achievements as an adult?		

3 On your own, write a definition of **prodigy.**

_____

_____

_____

4 Compile your classmates' responses to #3 on the board into a single definition.

_____

_____

_____

5 Below is the definition of a child prodigy. Compare this with your class's definition. Are the definitions similar or different? Explain your answer.

Child Prodigy: someone under the age of 13 who is capable of excelling in at least one area of skill at a level that is considered to be an adult level in that field. There are child prodigies in all different skill areas including music, math, chess, the arts and even humanities. As long as the child shows demonstrable adult-level skill in one of these areas prior to that age 13 mark, he or she is considered a prodigy in that area.

CD 1
Track 11

Are Gifted Children Born or Made?

by Susan Logue, *Voice of America News*

1   Some say given enough time, money and instruction, any child can develop a special expertise. Others, however, insist gifted children are born, not made.

A Rage to Master

Gaven Largent, 13, has been playing music for five years. He started with guitar lessons at age eight, but not long after, he quit—not making music, just
5   taking lessons. "I wasn't learning anything," he says. "I was just playing those notes on the paper; it was boring."

"Gaven became frustrated that it was sheet music and he was only playing the notes on the music," his mother Melissa says. "He wanted to fill it in and make it more." She says they knew when he was nine or ten that music would
10   be his focus. "It became an obsession for him to figure out the sounds that he heard on a CD or the radio or live music."

That obsession is one of the trademarks of a gifted child, or prodigy, according to developmental psychologist Ellen Winner, who teaches at Boston College. "I say they have a rage to master. It is difficult to tear them away from the area
15   in which they have high ability."

Looking Back as Former Child Prodigies

Julian Lage, who is now 21, remembers playing guitar for hours as a child. "You wake up and you eat and you play music and you sleep." Lage, who recently released his first CD, *Sounding Point*, started playing guitar at five. A few years later, he was the subject of a documentary film, *Jules at Eight*.

20 Still, the title "child prodigy" was something he never felt he could relate to. "Younger musicians, my contemporaries who have been called child prodigies, they feel slighted because it does undermine the work ethic, the thousands of hours you put in just to be able to produce a sound on your instrument."

25 That is a sentiment echoed by Rasta Thomas, 27, who was also labeled a prodigy. He made dance history as a teenager, winning the Gold Medal in the Senior Men's Division of the prestigious Jackson International Ballet Competition in Jackson, Mississippi at the age of 14. He now headlines his own dance company, Bad Boys of Dance. "I think if you give any seven-year-old the

30 training I had, you will get a product that is at the top of its game," Thomas says. "I have had hours and hours and a million dollars invested into the training that I received."

Enabling Talent to Flower

But Winner, the author of *Gifted Children: Myths and Realities*, disagrees. "You can't make a gifted child out of any child." Winner says prodigies are born with

35 natural talent, but she does believe they "need to be enabled in order to have their ability flower." Both Julian Lage, who played with vibraphonist Gary Burton at age 12, and Rasta Thomas, who studied at the Kirov Ballet Academy in Washington, say they had that support. But the success that both Lage and Thomas enjoy today as adults is due to much more. Winner says studies have

40 shown that most music prodigies are unheard of as adults. "The gift of being a child prodigy is very different from the gift of being an adult creator," she says. "To be an adult creator means you have to do something new, which means taking a risk." Both Lage and Thomas took that creative risk early, composing and choreographing while they were still in their teens. Gaven Largent is headed

45 in that direction as well. "I do write," he says. "I haven't written too many songs with lyrics, but that's something I'd like to work on." Right now, he adds, he is working on a gospel song.

Rasta Thomas performing with Adrienne Canterna in 1998. Today, the two former prodigies are married and still performing together.

Reading Overview: Main Idea, Details, Summary

Read the passage again. As you read, underline what you think are the most important ideas. Then, in one or two sentences, write the main idea of the reading. **Use your own words.**

Main Idea

_____

_____

_____

Details

Use the chart below to organize the information in the article. Refer back to the information you underlined in the passage as a guide. You will not fill in all the boxes on this chart. When you have finished, write a brief summary of the reading. **Use your own words.**

Are Gifted Children Born or Made?		
Name of psychologist:		
What is her profession?		
Does she believe gifted children are born or made? Why?		
Name of prodigy:	How does this person excel?	How does this person feel about being called a child prodigy? Why?
1.		
2.		
3.		

Summary

_____

_____

_____

B Statement Evaluation

Read the statements. Then scan the article to find out if each sentence is **True (T), False (F),** or an **Inference (I). Write T, F,** or **I.**

1 _____ People disagree on whether gifted children are born or made.

2 _____ Gaven Largent took guitar lessons for a long time.

3 _____ Ellen Winner believes that gifted children have a "rage to master."

4 _____ Julian Lage doesn't like being called a child prodigy.

5 _____ Julian Lage worked very hard to become successful.

6 _____ Rasta Thomas believes he is a successful dancer because he was a child prodigy.

7 _____ Most music prodigies do not become very successful as adults.

C Reading Analysis

Read each question carefully. Circle the letter or number of the correct answer, or write your answer.

1 In line 2, **expertise** means
   a. gift
   b. skill
   c. lesson

2 Read lines 3–6.

    a. **Not long after** means

        1. a short time later
        2. a long time later
        3. as soon as

    b. Why did Gaven quit taking lessons?

_____

3 Read lines 10–13.

    a. What was Gaven's **obsession?**

        1. taking guitar lessons
        2. playing the guitar
        3. figuring out the sounds he heard in music

    b. An **obsession** is

        1. a constant preoccupation with something
        2. an ability to learn something quickly
        3. a great love of music

    c. **Trademark** means

        1. a musical quality
        2. a unique characteristic
        3. a gifted child

4 Read lines 16–17. This means that Julian Lage

    a. never went to school
    b. didn't sleep a lot
    c. played music all day

5 Read lines 21–24.

    a. **Contemporaries** means

        1. classmates
        2. peers
        3. musicians

    b. Who are Julian's **contemporaries?**

_____

6 Read lines 29–30. What does **at the top of its game** mean?

    a. the winner of the game
    b. the best player of the game
    c. the highest level

7 Read lines 34–36. Winner believes child prodigies **need to be enabled to have their ability flower.** In this sentence, **flower** means

a. a kind of plant
b. grow
c. born

8 In lines 39–40, **Winner says studies have shown that most music prodigies are unheard of as adults.** This means

a. most music prodigies don't become famous when they're adults
b. most music prodigies don't want to hear music as adults
c. most music prodigies are unhappy as adults

Dictionary Skills

Read the excerpts from the article. Then read the dictionary entry for the boldfaced word and write the number of the definition that is appropriate for the context. Be prepared to explain your choice.

1 She says they knew when he was nine or 10 that music would be his **focus.**

focus: _____

> **focus** **1** **a :** a point at which rays (as of light, heat, or sound) converge or from which they diverge or appear to diverge; *specifically* **:** the point where the geometrical lines or their prolongations conforming to the rays diverging from or converging toward another point intersect and give rise to an image after reflection by a mirror or refraction by a lens or optical system **b :** a point of convergence of a beam of particles (as electrons) **2** **a :** FOCAL LENGTH **b :** adjustment for distinct vision; *also* **:** the area that may be seen distinctly or resolved into a clear image **c :** a state or condition permitting clear perception or understanding <tried to bring the issues into focus> **d :** DIRECTION <the team lost focus> ... **4** **:** a localized area of disease or the chief site of a generalized disease or infection **5** **a :** a center of activity, attraction, or attention <the focus of the meeting was drug abuse> **b :** a point of concentration....

2 A few years later, he was the **subject** of a documentary film, *Jules at Eight*.

subject: _____

> **subject** **1** : one that is placed under authority or control: as **a** : VASSAL **b** (1) : one subject to a monarch and governed by the monarch's law (2) : one who lives in the territory of, enjoys the protection of, and owes allegiance to a sovereign power or state... **3 a** : a department of knowledge or learning **b** : MOTIVE, CAUSE **c** (1) : one that is acted on <the helpless subject of their cruelty> (2) : an individual whose reactions or responses are studied (3) : a dead body for anatomical study and dissection **d** (1) : something concerning which something is said or done <the subject of the essay> (2) : something represented or indicated in a work of art **e** (1) : the term of a logical proposition that denotes the entity of which something is affirmed or denied; *also* : the entity denoted (2) : a word or word group denoting that of which something is predicated **f** : the principal melodic phrase on which a musical composition or movement is based

3 It is difficult to tear them away from the **area** in which they have high ability.

area: _____

> **area** **1** : a level piece of ground **2** : the surface included within a set of lines; *specifically* : the number of unit squares equal in measure to the surface—see METRIC SYSTEM TABLE, WEIGHT TABLE **3** : the scope of a concept, operation, or activity : FIELD <the whole area of foreign policy> ... **5** : a particular extent of space or surface or one serving a special function: as **a** : a part of the surface of the body **b** : a geographic region **6** : a part of the cerebral cortex having a particular function

4 Lage, who recently **released** his first CD, *Sounding Point*, started playing guitar at five.

release: _____

> **release** *transitive verb* **1** : to set free from restraint, confinement, or servitude <release hostages> <release pent-up emotions> <release the brakes>; *also* : to let go : DISMISS <*released* from her job> **2** : to relieve from something that confines, burdens, or oppresses <was *released* from her promise> **3** : to give up in favor of another : RELINQUISH <release a claim to property> **4** : to give permission for publication, performance, exhibition, or sale of; *also* : to make available to the public <the commission *released* its findings> <release a new movie>
> *intransitive verb* : to move from one's normal position (as in football or basketball) in order to assume another position or to perform a second assignment

Word Partnership   Use *subject* with:

adj.	**controversial** subject, **favorite** subject, **touchy** subject
n.	**knowledge of a** subject, subject **of a debate**, subject **of an investigation**, **research** subject, subject **of a sentence**, subject **of a verb**
v.	**broach a** subject, **study a** subject, **change the** subject
prep.	subject **to approval**, subject **to availability**, subject **to laws**, subject **to scrutiny**, subject **to a tax**

Word Partnership   Use *area* with:

adj.	**metropolitan** area, **rural/suburban/urban** area, **surrounding** area, **local** area, **remote** area, **residential** area, **restricted** area
n.	**downtown** area, **tourist** area
prep.	**throughout the** area, area **of expertise**

E Critical Thinking Strategies

Read each question carefully and write a response. Remember that there is no one correct answer. Your response depends on what **you** think.

1   Does Rasta Thomas believe he is successful because he was a child prodigy? Why or why not?

_____

_____

_____

By permission. From *Merriam-Webster's Collegiate® Dictionary*, 11th Edition © 2010 by Merriam-Webster, Incorporated (www.Merriam-Webster.com).

2 According to psychologist Ellen Winner, prodigies are born with natural talent, but need help to fully develop their potential. What do you think could prevent some child prodigies from being discovered or developed?

_____

_____

3 Is the special ability of child prodigies due to nature, nurture, or both? Explain your answer.

_____

_____

Alia Sabur (1989–): World's youngest university professor

Another Perspective

Read the article and answer the questions that follow.

CD 1
Track 12

Reading at 8 Months? That Was Just the Start

by Michael Winerip, *The New York Times*

1   Last month, Alia Sabur, a college senior, arrived at her final for Applied Math 301 at 7 P.M. The room was nearly empty. "What were you thinking?" asked her professor, Alan Tucker. The test was actually scheduled from 5 to 7:30 P.M.

Alia was thinking, "Time to get started." She sat down and finished in
5   15 minutes. Afterwards, her mother, Julie, recalls, "She looked very happy. I said, 'Alia, 15 minutes? Did you check it?' Alia said, 'It's fine, Mom.'" And it was. Another perfect score for Alia Sabur. . . .

Alia, who is 13 and will earn her undergraduate degree from the State University at Stony Brook this spring, has been stunning people for a long time,
10   beginning with her parents, who thought it odd when she started reading words at eight months old. Prof. Harold Metcalf had her in physics her freshman year. "I was skeptical," he says. "Such a little girl. Then the second or third class, she asked a question. I realized, this girl understands. I've occasionally seen this at 15 or 16, but not 10." And not just math and physics. She is also an accomplished
15   clarinetist. . . .

Her professors say that beyond an extraordinary mind, what makes Alia special is a hunger to learn, a willingness to work hard and an emotional balance well beyond her years. This would seem to be every parent's dream, but for a long time it was not. . . . By age five, Alia had finished the elementary reading
20   curriculum at her Long Island public school. By second grade, she traveled to middle school for eighth-grade math. ("The kids were so big," she recalled.)

Things fell apart in the fourth grade. Public school officials said they could no longer accommodate Alia's special needs, Ms. Sabur said, and even Manhattan's best private schools felt she was too advanced. Colleges they consulted would
25   not accept so young a child. . . . Finally, Ms. Sabur got help at Stony Brook. "Their attitude was, 'We're a public university, it's our duty to find a way,'" she said. The mother accompanied the ten-year-old to college every day. She never took notes in lectures—"The concepts are the important part," she said. . . .

Ms. Sabur knows what people think when they hear of her daughter. "They
think, 'social misfit,'" she said. Ms. Sabur has worked to help Alia find friends
her own age. Twice a week, she schedules an art class and lunch with a group
of ninth-grade girls. And while Alia said it felt a little forced at first—"I didn't
know a lot of the middle school stuff they were talking about"—she now counts
three of the girls as friends. . . . Charles Fortmann, Alia's research adviser, treats
her like a colleague. She is helping him with a project on protein folding that
could someday lead to a medical breakthrough. . . . He describes Alia as "a
quiet person, but you have to listen carefully. If she mentions a problem with
something I'm doing, there probably is." Alia is thinking of doing doctoral
research next year, attending a music conservatory and performing. . . .

1   Complete the chart with Alia's accomplishments and her age at the time.

Accomplishments	Age

2   What are two problems that Alia has had as a result of being a prodigy?
Describe the problems and the solutions in the chart below.

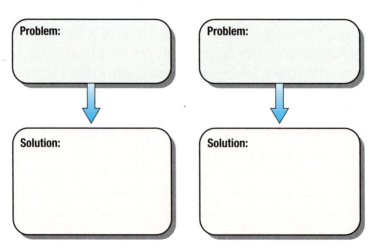

Problem:

Problem:

Solution:

Solution:

G Topics for Discussion and Writing

1. In this chapter, different people give their opinions about the question of whether prodigies are *born* or *made*. Whose opinion do you agree with? Why? Explain your answer.

2. Some extremely young child prodigies go to universities. Do you think this is a good environment for these children? Why or why not? Explain your answer, and give examples to support your opinion.

3. **Write in your journal.** Imagine you discover that your young son or daughter is a child prodigy. What will you do? How will you encourage your child? How will you protect your son or daughter's childhood?

H Follow-up Activities

1. Refer to the **Self-Evaluation of Reading Strategies** on the next page. Check off the strategies you used to understand "Are Gifted Children Born or Made?" Evaluate your strategy use over the first six chapters. Which strategies do you use consistently? Which strategies have you added to the list? Which strategies are becoming automatic? To what extent have you applied these strategies to other reading you do?

Self-Evaluation of Reading Strategies			
	Readings		
Strategies	"Who Lives Longer?"	"Switched at Birth"	"Are Gifted Children Born or Made?"
I read the title and try to predict what the reading will be about.			
I use my knowledge of the world to help me understand the text.			
I read as though I *expect* the text to have meaning.			
I use illustrations to help me understand the text.			
I ask myself questions about the text.			
I use a variety of types of context clues.			
I take chances in order to identify meaning.			
I continue if I am not successful.			
I identify and underline main ideas.			
I connect details with main ideas.			
I summarize the reading in my own words.			
I skip unnecessary words.			
I look up words correctly in the dictionary.			
I connect the reading to other material I have read.			
I do not translate into my native language.			

UNIT 2   INFLUENCES ON OUR LIVES: NATURE VERSUS NURTURE

2 Work with a partner. Choose one of the child prodigies discussed in this chapter. Write a list of questions that you would like to ask this child. Then, trade your list of questions with another pair of students. Have them answer your questions, while you and your partner answer their questions.

3 Child prodigies throughout history, and all over the world, show special talent in many areas: chess, music, and science, for example. In small groups, reread the passages about Mozart and Kim on pp. 99–100, and read the passage below. Describe each prodigy's special talent and the kind of life this person has or had. Then as a class, vote on the most talented prodigy.

William James Sidis

Do you know those people that you hear about primarily in fiction (or on TV shows) who are so smart that they go to college when they are still kids? That's the real life story of this boy who was born in New York City at the turn of the twentieth century and who was such a prodigy in both math and linguistics that he was accepted to attend Harvard University when he was only eleven years old. Interestingly, he strayed away from math entirely in his later years but is still considered to be one of the most intelligent people ever born.

William James Sidis (1898–1944)

Cloze Quiz

Complete the passage with words from the list. Use each word only once.

ability	difficult	lessons	radio
anything	expertise	music	remembers
boring	figure	obsession	title
born	focus	prodigy	undermine
contemporaries	frustrated	quit	wake

      Some say given enough time, money and instruction, any child can develop a special _____ (1) . Others, however, insist gifted children are _____ (2) , not made. Gaven Largent, 13, has been playing _____ (3) for five years. He started with guitar _____ (4) at age eight, but not long after, he _____ (5) , not making music, just taking lessons. "I wasn't learning _____ (6) ," he says. "I was just playing those notes on the paper; it was _____ (7) ."

    "Gaven became _____ (8) that it was sheet music and he was only playing the notes on the music," his mother Melissa says. She says they knew when he was nine or ten that music would be his _____ (9) . "It became an obsession for him to _____ (10) out the sounds that he heard on a CD or the _____ (11) or live music."

That _____ is one of the trademarks of a gifted child,
(12)

or _____ , according to developmental psychologist Ellen
(13)

Winner, who teaches at Boston College. "I say they have a rage to master. It is

_____ to tear them away from the area in which they have high
(14)

_____ ."
(15)

Julian Lage, who is now 21, _____ playing guitar for hours
(16)

as a child. "You _____ up and you eat and you play music and
(17)

you sleep." Lage started playing guitar at five. Still, the _____
(18)

"child prodigy" was something he never felt he could relate to. "Younger

musicians, my _____ who have been called child prodigies,
(19)

they feel slighted because it does _____ the work ethic, the
(20)

thousands of hours you put in just to be able to produce a sound on your

instrument."

Crossword Puzzle

Read the clues on the next page. Write the answers in the correct spaces in the puzzle.

Crossword Puzzle Clues

ACROSS CLUES

6. To exchange one for another

7. All-encompassing; deep

9. The opposite of **down**

10. The opposite of **no**

11. A very surprising or shocking fact

12. I want to _____ that. Don't throw it away.

15. An exceptionally bright child

16. Showing good sense

18. A change from one thing to another

21. Field

22. Skill

23. When you have a _____ , you have a voice in making a decision.

25. The past tense of **get**

29. An event marking a turning point

31. A group of related people; family

32. Shocked

33. When you _____ something, you become an expert.

34. The word _____ refers to the heart.

DOWN CLUES

1. Please wait _____ me.

2. One, _____ , three

3. Your peers; your equals

4. An unproved assertion

5. The opposite of **subtract**

6. Uncertainty

8. Untrue statements

13. A unique ability

14. To not eat

17. To wonder about; have doubts about

19. A social gathering

20. The opposite of **always**

24. Independence; control over one's life
26. A constant preoccupation with something
27. Grow; develop
28. Center of attention
30. Hold persistently in your mind
31. I _____ play the piano.

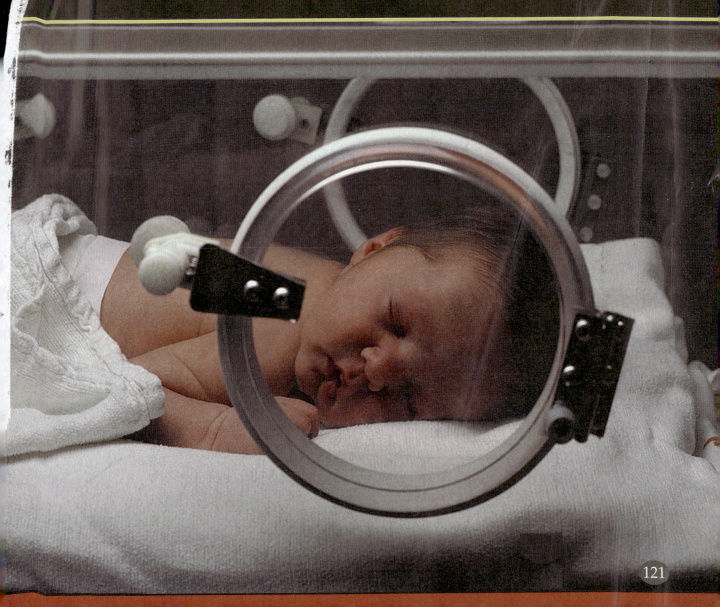

Technology and Ethical Issues

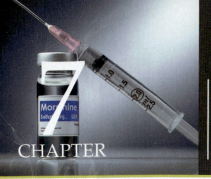

CHAPTER 7

Assisted Suicide: Multiple Perspectives

Prereading Preparation

1 This chapter presents a variety of perspectives on assisted suicide. Work with a partner or in a small group. Make a list of the different people who might have different viewpoints on assisted suicide. When you are finished, compare your list with your classmates' lists.

2 Dr. Timothy Quill of the University of Rochester has revealed publicly that he prescribed sleeping pills for Diane, a patient dying of leukemia, even though he knew she would use them to end her life. He discussed his decision with *U.S. News's* Amy Bernstein. Below are the questions that she asked him. With a partner, discuss what you think he replied, and write your answers. When you are finished, read Dr. Quill's actual answers on the next page.

Amy Bernstein's Questions:

a. How did you make your decision?

_____

_____

b. Have you had second thoughts, or doubts?

_____

_____

c. Do doctors often assist in suicides?

_____

_____

d. What are the legal consequences?

_____

_____

Dr. Quill's answers:

a. I knew Diane very well and was sure all avenues had been explored. Her alternatives were to tolerate increasing pain and fevers or to be heavily sedated—states worse than death. Sometimes, all one can look forward to is suffering, and our job is to try to lessen that in any way the patient wants. We may not be able to do some things because of personal beliefs, but the goal is to make the patient comfortable—and she defines what that entails, not the doctor.

b. I think about it a lot. I talked to a whole lot of people about it. But I think she got the best care possible.

c. Many doctors have a similar story—a secret about a very personal commitment to a patient that went to the edges of what's accepted.

d. It's a personal, not a legal, matter. This should be debated among clinicians and bioethicists. One purpose of what I did is to have that debate occur with a real case, with a real person who makes a very strong argument. Diane's gone. But there are many Dianes out there.

3 Compare your answers with the answers Dr. Quill gave Ms. Bernstein. Which answers were similar? Which were different?

4 As a member of the medical profession, Dr. Quill offers a particular perspective on assisted suicide. What other perspectives might a doctor have on this issue?

5 Read the excerpt on the next page from a book written by Dr. Francis Moore. When you finish reading, consider the viewpoints of both Dr. Quill and Dr. Moore. What do each of these doctors consider with regard to the issue of assisted suicide?

Matters of Life and Death

by Dr. Francis Moore, *National Academy of Sciences*

1   In a new book, *A Miracle and a Privilege,* Dr. Francis Moore, 81, of Harvard Medical School, discusses a lifetime of grappling with the issue of when to help a patient die. An excerpt:

Doctors of our generation are not newcomers to this question. Going back
5   to my internship days, I can remember many patients in pain, sometimes in a coma or delirious, with late, hopeless cancer. For many of them, we wrote an order for heavy medication—morphine[1] by the clock. This was not talked about openly and little was written about it. It was essential, not controversial.

10   The best way to bring the problem into focus is to describe two patients whom I cared for. The first, formerly a nurse, had sustained a fractured pelvis in an automobile accident. A few days later her lungs seemed to fill up; her urine stopped; her heart developed dangerous rhythm disturbances. So there she was: in a coma, on dialysis, on a breathing machine, her heartbeat maintained with an electrical device. One day after rounds, my secretary said the husband
15   and son of the patient wanted to see me. They told me their wife and mother was obviously going to die; she was a nurse and had told her family that she never wanted this kind of terrible death, being maintained by machines. I told them that while I respected their view, there was nothing intrinsically lethal about her situation. The kidney failure she had was just the kind for which
20   the artificial kidney was most effective. While possibly a bit reassured, they were disappointed. Here was the head surgeon, seemingly determined to keep everybody alive, no matter what.

When patients start to get very sick, they often seem to fall apart all at once.
25   The reverse is also true. Within a few days, the patient's pacemaker could be removed, and she awoke from her coma. About six months later I was again in my office. The door opened and in walked a gloriously fit woman. After some cheery words of appreciation, the father and son asked to speak to me alone. As soon as the door closed, both men became quite tearful. All that came out was,
30   "We want you to know how wrong we were."

[1] Morphine is a powerful narcotic. It can cause death in large doses (amounts).

The second patient was an 85-year-old lady whose hair caught fire while she was smoking. She arrived with a deep burn; I knew it would surely be fatal. As a remarkable coincidence, there was a seminar going on at the time in medical ethics, given by the wife of an official of our university. She asked me if I had any sort of ethical problem I could bring up for discussion. I described the case and asked the students their opinion. After the discussion, I made a remark that was, in retrospect, a serious mistake. I said, "I'll take the word back to the nurses about her, and we will talk about it some more before we decide." The instructor and the students were shocked: "You mean this is a real patient?" The teacher of ethics was not accustomed to being challenged by reality. In any event, I went back and met with the nurses. A day or two later, when she was making no progress and was suffering terribly, we began to back off treatment. When she complained of pain, we gave her plenty of morphine. A great plenty. Soon she died quietly and not in pain. As a reasonable physician, you had better move ahead and do what you would want done for you. And don't discuss it with the world first. There is a lesson here for everybody. Assisting people to leave this life requires strong judgment and long experience to avoid its misuse.

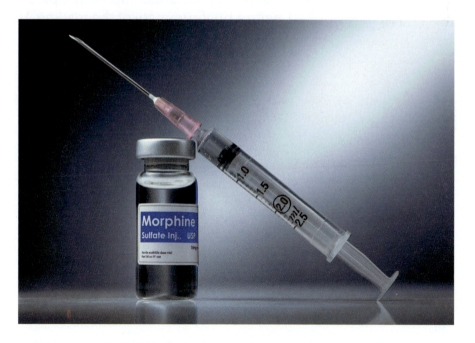

Reading Overview: Main Idea, Details, and Summary

Read the passage again. As you read, underline what you think are the most important ideas. Then, in one or two sentences, write the main idea of the reading. **Use your own words.**

Main Idea

_____

_____

_____

Details

Use the flowchart on the next page to organize the information in this article. Refer back to the information you underlined in the passage as a guide. When you have finished, write a brief summary of the reading. **Use your own words.**

MATTERS OF LIFE AND DEATH

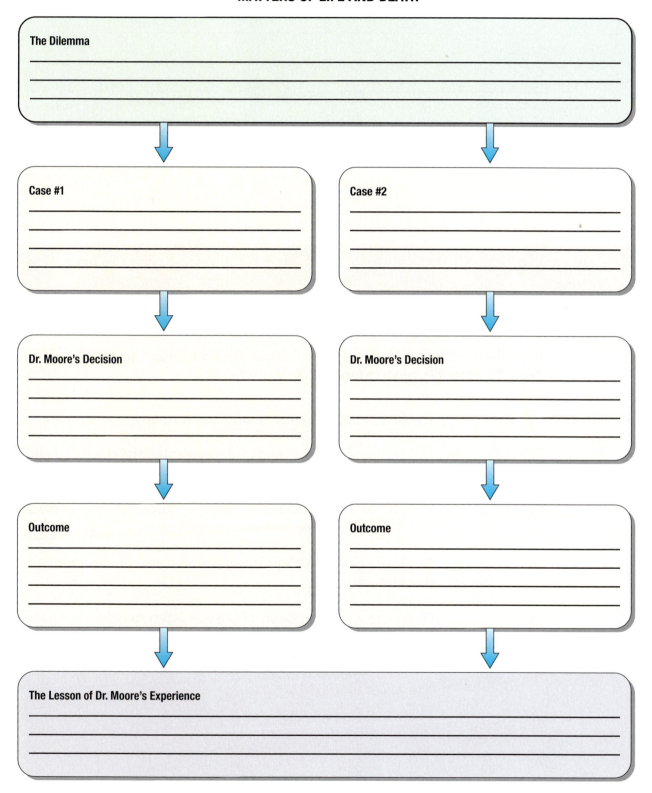

The Dilemma
_____
_____
_____

Case #1
_____
_____
_____
_____

Case #2
_____
_____
_____
_____

Dr. Moore's Decision
_____
_____
_____
_____

Dr. Moore's Decision
_____
_____
_____
_____

Outcome
_____
_____
_____

Outcome
_____
_____
_____

The Lesson of Dr. Moore's Experience
_____
_____
_____

Summary

_____

_____

_____

_____

_____

B

Statement Evaluation

Read the statements. Then scan the article to find out if each sentence is
True (T), False (F), or an **Inference (I).** Write **T, F** or **I.**

1 _____ The first patient discussed, who was formerly a nurse, died.

2 _____ The first patient's husband and son wanted the doctor to end
her life.

3 _____ The instructor and students were very surprised that Dr. Moore
was discussing a real patient.

4 _____ Dr. Moore gave the 85-year-old woman enough morphine so
that she would die.

5 _____ Dr. Moore would probably choose assisted suicide if he should
become terminally ill.

Reading Analysis

Read each question carefully. Circle the letter or number of the correct answer, or write your answer.

1 Read lines 1–6.

   a. An **excerpt** is

      1. an example of an issue
      2. a part of a longer reading
      3. an introduction to a book

   b. **Doctors of our generation** refers to

      1. old doctors
      2. young doctors
      3. doctors about the same age as the author

   c. What does **this question** refer to?

   _____

   d. **My internship days** refers to

      1. the time when the author was younger
      2. a time in the recent past
      3. the time when the author was training as a doctor

2 Read lines 8–9: **It was essential, not controversial.**

   a. What was **essential?**

   _____

   b. **Essential** means

      1. necessary
      2. medicine
      3. expensive

   c. **Controversial** refers to

      1. something people agree on
      2. something people argue about
      3. something people have to do

3 Read lines 15–16. **Rounds** refers to

   a. circular motions
   b. when doctors go around a hospital visiting their patients
   c. when a person is put on a breathing machine

4 Read lines 18–20. **There was nothing intrinsically lethal about her situation** means

    a. the woman's condition was fatal

    b. the woman's condition was not fatal

5 Read lines 24–27.

    a. What does **the reverse is also true** mean?

    _____

    b. Read lines 12–13 and lines 25–26. What is a **pacemaker?**

    _____

    c. How do you know?

    _____

6 Read line 27. Who was the **gloriously fit woman?**

_____

_____

7 Read lines 31–33. **I knew it would surely be fatal** means

    a. the doctor thought the patient might live

    b. the doctor thought the patient might die

    c. the doctor knew the patient would die

8 Read lines 36–41.

    a. **In retrospect** means

        1. looking at something seriously

        2. looking sadly at something

        3. looking back at a past situation

    b. **In any event** means

        1. anyway

        2. however

        3. in addition

9 Read line 46. **Don't discuss it with the world first** means

    a. don't talk about your patients at seminars

    b. don't talk about your patients with nurses

    c. don't talk to many people about your patients

Dictionary Skills

Read the excerpts from the article. Then read the dictionary entry for the boldfaced word and write the number of the definition that is appropriate for the context. Be prepared to explain your choice.

1 There was a seminar going on at the time in medical **ethics,** given by the wife of an official of our university.

ethic: _____

> **ethic** **1** *plural but sing. or plural in constr.* **:** the discipline dealing with what is good and bad and with moral duty and obligation **2 a :** a set of moral principles **:** a theory or system of moral values <the present-day materialistic ethic> <an old-fashioned work ethic> —often used in plural but singular or plural in construction <an elaborate ethics> <Christian ethics> **b** *plural but sing. or plural in constr.* **:** the principles of conduct governing an individual or a group <professional ethics> **c :** a guiding philosophy **d :** a consciousness of moral importance <forge a conservation ethic> **3** *plural* **:** a set of moral issues or aspects (as rightness) <debated the ethics of human cloning>

2 The first patient had sustained a **fractured** pelvis in an automobile accident.

fracture: _____

> **fracture** **1 a :** to cause a fracture in **:** BREAK <fracture a rib> **b :** RUPTURE, TEAR **2 a :** to damage or destroy as if by rupturing **b :** to cause great disorder in **c :** to break up **:** FRACTIONATE **d :** to go beyond the limits of (as rules) **:** VIOLATE <*fractured* the English language with malaprops — Goodman Ace> . . .

By permission. From *Merriam-Webster's Collegiate® Dictionary*, 11th Edition © 2010 by Merriam-Webster, Incorporated (www.Merriam-Webster.com).

3 The patient's heartbeat was **maintained** with an electrical device (a pacemaker).

The man and his son told me their wife and mother was obviously going to die; she had told her family that she never wanted this kind of terrible death, being **maintained** by machines.

maintain: _____

> **maintain** **1** : to keep in an existing state (as of repair, efficiency, or validity) : preserve from failure or decline <maintain machinery> **2** : to sustain against opposition or danger : uphold and defend <maintain a position> **3** : to continue or persevere in : CARRY ON, KEEP UP <couldn't maintain his composure> **4** **a** : to support or provide for <has a family to maintain> **b** : SUSTAIN <enough food to maintain life> **5** : to affirm in or as if in argument : ASSERT <maintained that the earth is flat>

4 The first patient had **sustained** a fractured pelvis in an automobile accident.

sustain: _____

> **sustain** **1** : to give support or relief to **2** : to supply with sustenance : NOURISH **3** : KEEP UP, PROLONG . . . **5** : to buoy up <sustained by hope> **6** **a** : to bear up under **b** : SUFFER, UNDERGO <sustained heavy losses> **7** **a** : to support as true, legal, or just **b** : to allow or admit as valid <the court sustained the motion> **8** : to support by adequate proof : CONFIRM <testimony that sustains our contention>

Word Link

fract, frag = breaking : fraction, fracture, fragile

Word Partnership   Use *maintain* with:

n.	maintain **friendship**, maintain **law**, maintain **a relationship**
v.	**need to** maintain, **pledge to** maintain, **try to** maintain

---

Critical Thinking Strategies

Read each question carefully, and write a response. Remember that there is no one correct answer. Your response depends on what **you** think.

1 Reread Dr. Quill's answer to Amy Bernstein's fourth question. Consider his response with regard to Dr. Moore's experience in the medical ethics seminar. Do you think Dr. Moore and Dr. Quill would agree on the matter of debating the ethics of assisted suicide? Explain your answer.

_____

_____

_____

_____

_____

2 What did the husband and the son of the former nurse want the doctor to do? Why were they disappointed?

_____

_____

_____

3 When the father and son revisited him, Dr. Moore states that **both men became quite tearful.** Why do you think they reacted this way?

_____

_____

_____

4 Why did the doctors give the 85-year-old woman **plenty of morphine**? What does Dr. Moore mean by **a great plenty?**

_____

_____

_____

5 In giving advice, Dr. Moore states, **And don't discuss it with the world first.** What does **it** refer to? Why does Dr. Moore say not to discuss **it** with the world?

_____

_____

_____

_____

_____

UNIT 3   TECHNOLOGY AND ETHICAL ISSUES

Another Perspective

Read the article and answer the questions that follow.

CD 2
Track 02

Should Doctors Be Allowed to Help Terminally Ill Patients Commit Suicide?

by Derek Humphry and Daniel Callahan, *Health*

YES

It would be a great comfort to people who face terminal illness to know they could get help to die if their suffering became unbearable. All pain cannot be controlled, and it's arrogant for anybody to say that it can. Quality of life decisions are the sole right of the individual.

It's nonsense to say that death shouldn't be part of a doctor's job—it already is. We all die. Death is a part of medicine. One of a doctor's jobs is to write death certificates. So this idea of the doctor as superhealer is a load of nonsense. The fact is that it's not so easy to commit suicide on your own. It's very hard for decent citizens to get deadly drugs. Even if they do, there's the fear that the drugs won't work. There are hundreds of dying people who couldn't lift their hand to their mouth with a cup of coffee, let alone a cup of drugs. They need assistance.

NO

If it's a question of someone's wanting the right to die, I say jump off a building. But as soon as you bring in somebody else to help you, it changes the equation. Suicide is legally available to people in this country. Just don't ask a doctor to help you do it. That would violate the traditions of medicine and raise doubts about the role of the physician.

One of my worries is that people will be manipulated by a doctor's suggesting suicide. A lot of seriously ill people already feel they're a burden because they're costing their families money. It would be easy for a family to insinuate, "While we love you, Grandmother, and we're willing to spend all our money and not send the kids to college, wouldn't it be better if . . . ?" There is no coercion there, but you build on somebody's guilt. We'd have a whole new class of

1

5

10

15

20

Of course, people who are depressed or who feel they are a weight on their families should be counseled and helped to live. But you have to separate those instances from people who are dying, whose bodies are giving up on them. If you think there is a cure around the corner for your malady, then please wait for it. That is your choice. But sometimes a person realizes that her life is coming to an end, as in the case of my wife, whose doctor said, "There is nothing else we can do."

We're not talking about cases in which a depressed person will come to a doctor and ask to be killed. Under the law the Hemlock Society is trying to get passed, the doctor must say *no* to depressed people. A candidate for assisted suicide has to be irreversibly, terminally, hopelessly ill and judged to be so by two doctors.

Derek Humphry is the founder of the Hemlock Society and author of Final Exit, *a book advising terminally ill people on how to commit suicide.*

people considering suicide who hadn't thought about it before.

Then, too, I don't believe that you could successfully regulate this practice. The relationship between the doctor and the patient begins in confidentiality. If they decide together that they don't want anybody to know, there is no way the government can regulate it. The presumption is that physicians would only be helping people commit suicide after everything else had failed to end their suffering. But a lot of people won't want to be that far along. None of the proposed regulations takes into account a person who is not suffering now, but who says, "I don't want to suffer in the future. Let me commit suicide now." I can imagine a doctor who would say, "Yes, we're going to make sure that you don't have to suffer at all."

Daniel Callahan is a bioethicist and director of the Hastings Center, a medical ethics think tank in Briarcliff Manor, New York.

1 Describe Derek Humphry's position on doctor-assisted suicide for

a. terminally ill people

_____

_____

b. depressed people

_____

_____

2 What do you think happened to Derek Humphry's wife? Explain your answer.

_____

_____

_____

3 Describe Daniel Callahan's position on doctor-assisted suicide for terminally ill people.

_____

_____

4 What are some reasons that Daniel Callahan gives for his opinion?

_____

_____

_____

G Topics for Discussion and Writing

1 In the United States, some people write a "living will" before their death. A "living will" can prevent doctors from prolonging a person's life if he or she becomes seriously ill. For example, the person may not want to be resuscitated if he or she stops breathing, or placed on a respirator or feeding tube if he or she cannot breathe or eat on his or her own. Would you want to write a "living will"? If not, why not? If so, under what conditions would you want to be allowed to die naturally? Write a composition explaining your answer.

2 What is your opinion on doctor-assisted suicide? Should it be legal? Should it be banned? Write a paragraph stating your opinion. Then discuss your opinion with your classmates.

3 **Write in your journal.** If someone you loved were terminally ill and wanted his or her doctor to perform an assisted suicide, would you approve? Would you encourage the doctor to agree to assist in the suicide? Explain your answer.

Follow-up Activities

1. Refer to the **Self-Evaluation of Reading Strategies** on page 178. Check off the strategies you used to understand "Matters of Life and Death." Think about the strategies you didn't use, and apply them to help you understand the readings that follow.

2. Work with one or two classmates. Review the various perspectives given by the authors in this chapter. Whose perspectives were included? Whose perspectives were omitted? What perspectives might these excluded people have? Make a list of these people and their possible perspectives, and discuss them with the class.

3. a. Work in groups of three or four students. Discuss the following case.

   Martin is a 40-year-old father of two young children. He was recently involved in a serious car accident and was critically injured. The doctors have declared him "brain dead," which means that his brain does not show any mental activity at all. He is being kept alive on a feeding tube and a respirator that breathes for him because he cannot breathe on his own. The doctors do not believe he will ever improve. However, he could be kept alive, but unconscious, on the machines indefinitely. The family must make an extremely difficult decision: Should they continue to keep Martin on these machines in the hospital, which is costing thousands of dollars a day, or should they allow him to die? Although Martin's family does not have a lot of money, they love him very much. What do you think they should do? What might be the consequences of this decision?

   b. As a class, form a medical ethics committee. Discuss each group's decision and the possible consequences. Then decide what you think Martin's family should do.

   c. Think about how you came to your decision. What factors or values influenced your decision?

Cloze Quiz

Complete the passage with words from the list. Use each word only once.

awoke	fatal	machines	respected
case	fractured	maintained	sick
describe	in retrospect	medication	smoking
essential	internship	problem	students
ethics	lethal	reality	their

Doctors of our generation are not newcomers to this question. Going back to my _____ days, I can remember many patients in
(1)
pain, sometimes in a coma, with late, hopeless cancer. For many of them, we wrote an order for heavy _____—morphine by the clock.
(2)
This was not talked about openly, and little was written about it. It was _____ not controversial.
(3)

The best way to bring the problem into focus is to _____
(4)
two patients whom I cared for. The first, formerly a nurse, had sustained a _____ pelvis in an automobile accident. A few days later her
(5)
lungs seemed to fill up; her heart developed dangerous rhythm disturbances. So there she was: in a coma, on a breathing machine, her heartbeat _____ with an electrical device. One day the husband and son
(6)
of the patient came to see me. They told me _____ wife and
(7)
mother was obviously going to die; she had told her family that she never wanted this kind of terrible death, being maintained by _____ .
(8)
I told them that while I _____ their view, there was nothing
(9)
intrinsically _____ about her situation. While possibly a bit
(10)
reassured, they were disappointed.

When patients start to get very _____(11)_____ they often seem to fall apart all at once. The reverse is also true. Within a few days, the patient's pacemaker could be removed and she _____(12)_____ from her coma.

The second patient was an 85-year-old lady whose hair caught fire while she was _____(13)_____ . She arrived with a deep burn; I knew it would surely be _____(14)_____ . As a remarkable coincidence, there was a seminar going on at the time in medical _____(15)_____ given by the wife of an official of our university. She asked me if I had any sort of ethical _____(16)_____ I could bring up for discussion. I described the _____(17)_____ and asked the students their opinion. After the discussion, I made a remark that was, _____(18)_____ a serious mistake. I said, "I'll take the word back to the nurses about her, and we will talk about it some more before we decide." The instructor and the _____(19)_____ were shocked: "You mean this is a real patient?" The teacher of ethics was not accustomed to being challenged by _____(20)_____ .

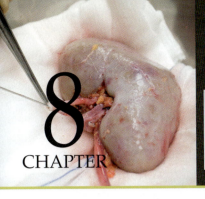

8
CHAPTER

Sales of Kidneys Prompt New Laws and Debate

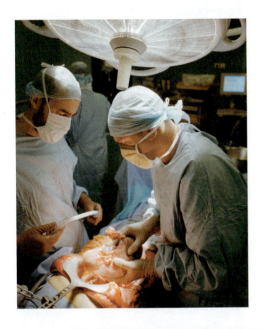

Prereading Preparation

Read the following article. Then complete the survey and answer the questions that follow.

CD 2
Track 03

Trading Flesh Around the Globe

Time

1   A ghoulish[1] notion: people so poor that they sell some of their body parts to survive. But for scores of brokers who buy and sell human organs in Asia, Latin America and Europe, that theme from a late-night horror movie is merely a matter of supply and demand. There are thousands more patients
5   in need of kidneys, corneas, skin grafts and other human tissue than there are donors; therefore, big money can be made on a thriving black market in human flesh.

[1] *Ghoulish* is the adjective form of *ghoul,* which refers to a legendary evil creature that robs graves and eats the dead. It is an extremely negative word.

In India, the going rate for a kidney from a live donor is $1,500; for a cornea, $4,000; for a patch of skin, $50. Two centers of the thriving kidney trade are Bombay, where private clinics cater to Indians and a foreign clientele dominated by wealthy Arabs, and Madras, a center for patients from Malaysia, Singapore and Thailand. Renal patients in India and Pakistan who cannot find a relative to donate a kidney are permitted to buy newspaper advertisements offering living donors up to $4,300 for the organ. Mohammad Aqeel, a poor Karachi tailor who recently sold one of his kidneys for $2,600, said he needed the money "for the marriage of two daughters and paying off of debts."

In India, Africa, Latin America, and Eastern Europe, young people advertise organs for sale, sometimes to pay for college educations. In Hong Kong a businessman named Tsui Fung circulated a letter to doctors in March offering to serve as middleman between patients seeking the kidney transplants and a Chinese military hospital in Nanjing that performs the operation. The letter said the kidneys would come from live "volunteers," implying that they would be paid donors. The fee for the kidney, the operation and round-trip airfare: $12,800.

1 Work in small groups and answer the following survey about selling organs. When you are finished, compile the answers on the board.

Would you sell:	Student 1	Student 2	Student 3	Student 4
one of your kidneys?	Yes / No	Yes / No	Yes / No	Yes / No
one of your corneas?	Yes / No	Yes / No	Yes / No	Yes / No
a patch of your skin?	Yes / No	Yes / No	Yes / No	Yes / No
a lobe from your lung?	Yes / No	Yes / No	Yes / No	Yes / No

2 Look at the results of your class survey. What are the conditions under which your classmates would sell their organs? Ask the students who answered *yes* to complete the following statement:

I would sell _____ for the following reasons:

_____

_____

3 Read the title of this article. What new laws and what debate do you think the sale of kidneys has prompted?

_____

_____

_____

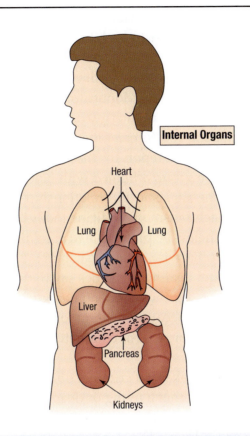

Internal Organs

Heart

Lung   Lung

Liver

Pancreas

Kidneys

CD 2
Track 04

Sales of Kidneys Prompt New Laws and Debate

by Terry Trucco, *The New York Times*

1   Last summer Colin Benton died after receiving a kidney transplant at a private London hospital. Several months later, however, his case made headlines throughout Britain when his widow disclosed that her husband's kidney transplant had come from a Turkish citizen who was paid $3,300 to fly to Britain

and donate the organ. The donor said he had decided to sell his kidney to pay for medical treatment for his daughter. Concern in Britain over issues raised in the case resulted in a law passed on July 28, 1989, in Parliament banning the sale of human organs for transplant.

The same concerns and those over loopholes in the transplant laws in some other nations led the World Health Organization to condemn the practice recently. In a resolution in May, the organization asked member nations to take appropriate measures, including legislation, to prohibit trafficking in human organs.

But as Britain was moving to make the sale of human organs unlawful, as it is in the United States, ethicists and policy analysts in the United States were beginning to suggest that paying donors, or their estates, may be an effective way to increase the supply of organs available for transplant.

The idea of organs for sale "is creeping into health care discussions," Joel L. Swerdlow said in a recent report for the Annenberg Washington Program, a public policy research group affiliated with Northwestern University in Evanston, Illinois. "The altruistic 'gift relationship' may be inadequate as a motivator and an anachronism in medicine today," he wrote. "If paying seems wrong, it may nevertheless be preferable to accepting the suffering and death of patients who cannot otherwise obtain transplants."

Doctors, lawyers and health authorities say the sale of organs by impoverished donors is a growing phenomenon. Because it is possible to live with just one kidney and because demand for the organs is so high, kidneys are among the most popular organs for commercial transactions. People have sold their own blood for years.

The new British law makes it a criminal offense to give or receive money for supplying organs of either a living or dead person. It also prohibits acting as a broker in such an arrangement, advertising for organs for payment or transplanting an organ from a live donor not closely related to the recipient.

A new computerized nationwide registry, which records all transplants from both live donors and cadavers, will be used to help enforce the law. Punishment for breaking the law is either a $3,300 fine or three months in prison. Doctors convicted under the law could lose their right to practice medicine.

The health organization's resolution calls for compiling information on organ trafficking laws in member countries and publicizing the findings. At least 20 other countries, including the United States, Canada and most of Western Europe, already have laws or policies prohibiting the sale of human organs.

Britain has had a transplant law since the 1961 Human Tissue Act, which deemed it unethical for a practitioner to traffic in human organs. But the new law is believed to be the world's first legislation aimed exclusively at the commercial organ transactions. The British law applies only to transplants performed in the nation's private hospitals and not to those overseen by the government-supported National Health Service, which provides free medical care for British citizens. The service, which has not used paid donors, gets first pick of all kidneys available for transplant in the nation. At present, about 1,600 transplants are performed each year, with a waiting list of about 3,600 patients.

But, as in the United States, many patients from countries without high-quality kidney care come to Britain each year to undergo transplants in private hospitals. These hospitals rely on cadaver kidneys or live donor transplants from relatives of patients.

In the past, doctors simply questioned foreign donors to make certain they were related to recipients, but most admit the system was hardly foolproof. Often doctors could not communicate with patients who did not speak English. A doctor involved in the Benton case said he attempted to find out if the donor had been paid by waving a 5-pound note at him. "A number of us were duped by patients with forged medical referrals and documents saying they were relatives," said Maurice Slapak, director of a hospital transplant unit in Britain.

Despite the speed and ease with which the British transplant law was passed, it remains controversial. In a letter to *The Times* of London, Royden Harrison, professor emeritus at Warwick University, wrote: "What possible objection can there be if one person, of their own free will, should sell their kidney to someone else? The seller is able to indulge in a few of the good things in life. The buyer may well be paying to survive." Sir Michael McNair Wilson, a member of Parliament who is on a waiting list for a new kidney, has argued that selling a kidney is like women in the nineteenth century selling their hair. "As someone waiting to receive a transplant, I would only like to feel that the organ I am given is a gift from someone," he said. "But while there is a shortage of kidneys, I do not see why it is wrong for you to do what you will with your body."

"If it takes $25,000 to $30,000 annually to keep someone alive on an artificial kidney machine," John M. Newman wrote in the Annenberg Program report, "government payment of, for example, $5,000 for transplantable cadaver kidneys (even with the cost of transportation), would still make successful kidney transplantation cost effective." Dr. Newman, a kidney transplant recipient, is a director of the American Association of Kidney Patients. "This is not to suggest that a monetary value can be placed on human life or on life-saving organs," he added. "This does suggest, however, that a monetary 'thank you' from the federal government could stimulate increases in organ and tissue availability for transplantation and research."

There is concern that the new law could scare off suitable donors and add to the shortage of kidneys by somehow creating the impression that all donations are improper. A report by the National Kidney Research Fund said there had been a dramatic fall in the number of kidney donations earlier this year following the kidney-for-sale controversy. "There have effectively been at least 100 fewer transplant operations this year, and that means 100 people may have died because of the unfavorable publicity," the organization said in a statement.

Some opponents of the law simply think that it is addressing the wrong health issue. Elizabeth Ward, founder of the British Kidney Patients Association, supports legislation that would make organ donation automatic upon death. Those who choose not to donate would have to make a formal request. But Belgium began such a program several years ago, and it has had little effect. Doctors are reluctant to use the law. Doctors still ask next of kin for permission to remove organs. It's a moral issue. Nevertheless, many in the medical profession think the law was needed.

"If we take the very extreme view, people in desperate circumstances might be prepared to martyr themselves, selling their hearts to save their families," said Ross Taylor, director of transplant surgery at the Royal Victoria Infirmary in Newcastle upon Tyne and president of the British Transplantation Society. Mr. Taylor also criticized those tempted to sell their organs for frivolous reasons. "I have met people prepared to sell their kidneys to buy Porsches or to take a girlfriend on a holiday."

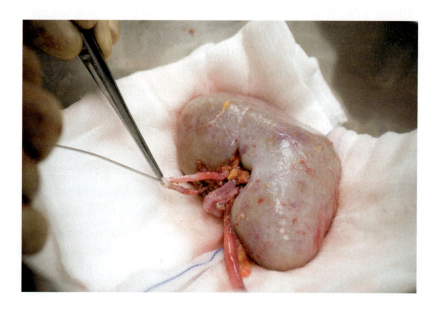

Reading Overview: Main Idea, Details, and Summary

Read the passage again. As you read, underline what you think are the most important ideas. Then, in one or two sentences, write the main idea of the reading. **Use your own words.**

Main Idea

_____

_____

_____

Details

Use the outline to organize the information in the article. Refer back to the information you underlined in the passage as a guide. Not all the boxes will be filled in. When you have finished, write a brief summary of the reading. **Use your own words.**

	Britain	World Health Organization	United States of America	Belgium
Laws about organ donation				
Opinions about sales of organs				
Arguments in favor of a law prohibiting the sale of organs	1. 2. 3.			
Arguments against a law prohibiting the sale of organs	1. 2. 3.			

Summary

_____

_____

_____

_____

B

Statement Evaluation

Read the statements. Then scan the article to find out if each sentence is
True (T), False (F), or **Not Mentioned (NM)** in the article. Write **T, F,** or **NM.**

1 _____ In Britain it is legal to sell organs.

2 _____ The World Health Organization supports the sale of organs for
transplants.

3 _____ In the United States it is unlawful to sell organs.

4 _____ Some policy analysts in the United States think that paying
donors may increase the number of organ transplants.

5 _____ Most of Asia already has laws prohibiting the sale of
human organs.

6 _____ In Britain organ donation is automatic when someone dies.

7 _____ Dr. John M. Newman paid the person who donated a kidney
to him.

8 _____ In Belgium organ donation is automatic when someone dies.

Reading Analysis

Read each question carefully. Circle the letter or number of the correct answer, or write the answer.

1 Read lines 1–8.

   a. Who is the **donor?**

      1. The person who receives the organ
      2. The person who gives the organ

   b. In the sentence, **Concern in Britain over issues raised in the case . . . ,** what is one of the **issues** in this **case?**

      1. Colin Benton's kidney donor was paid $3,300.
      2. Colin Benton died after his kidney transplant.

2 Read lines 9–12.

   a. What does **the practice** refer to?

_____

   b. **To prohibit trafficking in human organs** means

      1. to allow the buying and selling of human organs
      2. to forbid the buying and selling of human organs
      3. to control the buying and selling of human organs

3 Read lines 24–25. **Impoverished donors** are

   a. healthy
   b. important
   c. poor

4 Read lines 44–48.

   a. In the sentence, **The service . . . gets first pick . . . ,** what is **the service?**

_____

   b. **Gets first pick** means the service

      1. has first choice of the available kidneys
      2. can decide which hospital gets kidneys

5 Read lines 52–53.

    a. What are **live donors** and **cadavers?**

        1. Opposites

        2. Synonyms

    b. What is a **cadaver?**

        1. A donor

        2. An organ

        3. A dead body

6 Read lines 73–77. **$5,000 for transplantable cadaver kidneys . . . would still make successful kidney transplantation cost effective** means

    a. it's less expensive to pay a donor for a kidney than it is to keep someone alive on an artificial kidney machine

    b. it's less expensive to keep someone alive on an artificial kidney machine than it is to pay a donor for a kidney

7 Read lines 95–96. Who are **next of kin?**

    a. Lawyers

    b. Other doctors

    c. Family members

8 Read lines 98–104.

    a. What does **to martyr themselves** mean?

        1. To die

        2. To undergo an operation

        3. To put themselves in danger

    b. What are examples of **frivolous reasons** why people might sell their organs?

    _____

    c. What does **frivolous** mean?

        1. Exciting; fun

        2. Minor; trivial

        3. Expensive; costly

D Dictionary Skills

Read the excerpts from the article. Then read the dictionary entry for the boldfaced word and write the number of the definition that is appropriate for the context. Be prepared to explain your choice.

1 Some opponents of the British transplant law think that it **addresses** the wrong health issue.

address: _____

> **address** *transitive verb* **1** *archaic* **a :** DIRECT, AIM **b :** to direct to go : SEND **2 a :** to direct the efforts or attention of (oneself) <will address himself to the problem> **b :** to deal with : TREAT <intrigued by the chance to address important issues — I. L. Horowitz> **3** *archaic :* to make ready; *especially :* DRESS **4 a :** to communicate directly <addresses his thanks to his host> **b :** to speak or write directly to; *especially :* to deliver a formal speech to **5 a :** to mark directions for delivery on <address a letter> **b :** to consign to the care of another (as an agent or factor). . .

2 Colin Benton's case made headlines when his widow **disclosed** that his kidney transplant had come from a Turkish citizen.

disclose: _____

> **disclose** **1** *obsolete :* to open up **2 a :** to expose to view **b** *archaic :* HATCH **c :** to make known or public <demands that politicians disclose the sources of their income>

3 **a.** The World Health Organization recently condemned the **practice** of selling human organs for transplant.

b. Doctors who are convicted under the British transplant law may lose their medical license and their **practice.**

practice: (a) _____ (b) _____

> **practice** **1** **a** : actual performance or application <ready to carry out in practice what they advocated in principle> **b** : a repeated or customary action <had this irritating practice> **c** : the usual way of doing something <local practices> **d** : the form, manner, and order of conducting legal suits and prosecutions **2** **a** : systematic exercise for proficiency <practice makes perfect> **b** : the condition of being proficient through systematic exercise <get in practice> **3** **a** : the continuous exercise of a profession **b** : a professional business; *especially* : one constituting an incorporeal property

4 The World Health Organization wants member nations to create legislation that would make it illegal to **traffic in** human organs. In fact, Britain's transplant law deems it unethical for a practitioner to **traffic in** any human organs.

traffic in: _____

> **traffic** *intransitive verb* **1** : to carry on traffic **2** : to concentrate one's effort or interest; *broadly* : ENGAGE, DEAL <a writer who often traffics in hyperbole>
> *transitive verb* **1** **a** : to travel over <heavily *trafficked* highways> **b** : to visit as a customer <a highly *trafficked* bookstore> **2** : TRADE, BARTER

Word Partnership	Use *address* with:	
adj.	**permanent** address, **public** address, **inaugural** address	
n.	**name and** address, **street** address, address **remarks to**	

Word Partnership	Use *practice* with:	
prep.	**after** practice, **during** practice	
adj.	**clinical** practice, **legal** practice, **medical** practice, **private** practice	

Critical Thinking Strategies

Read each question carefully, and write a response. Remember that there is no one correct answer. Your response depends on what **you** think.

1 Does the author present the information in the article subjectively or objectively? Explain the reasons for your answer.

_____

_____

_____

2 How do you think Terry Trucco, the journalist who wrote the article, feels about this issue? What makes you think this?

_____

_____

_____

3 Refer to the case of Colin Benton.

a. Why did Mrs. Benton's disclosure make headlines throughout Britain?

_____

_____

b. What issues were raised as a result of this case?

_____

_____

4 Compare the growing attitude in the United States to the new legislation in Britain. How are the policies of the two countries changing?

_____

_____

_____

5 Both Sir Michael McNair Wilson and Dr. John M. Newman are in favor of the sale of human organs for transplants. What do you think might be some reasons for their opinions?

_____

_____

_____

6 Sir Michael McNair Wilson has argued that selling a kidney is like women in the nineteenth century selling their hair. Do you think this is a reasonable comparison? Explain your answer.

_____

_____

_____

7 Elizabeth Ward suggests that organ donation should be made automatic upon death unless an individual specifically requests otherwise. Why does she think this is a better approach to the issue of organ donations than Britain's new law is?

_____

_____

_____

Topics for Discussion and Writing

1 In the United States, it is illegal to sell or buy organs. Do you think that governments have the right or the responsibility to make laws controlling the sale of organs? What are your reasons? Do you think it is wrong to buy or sell organs? Should this be a legal issue or a moral issue? Why or why not? Discuss your opinions with your classmates.

2 In Belgium, when a person dies, his or her organs are automatically donated unless that person had formally requested not to be a donor before he or she died. Do you think this is a good program? Would you want to donate your organs after your death? Why or why not? Write a paragraph explaining your answer.

3 In 2009, 16,500 kidney transplants were performed in the United States. Approximately 6,000 kidneys came from living donors, and 10,500 came from deceased donors. What do you think can be done to encourage more people to donate a kidney while they are alive? After their death?

4 Do you think the sale of organs from live donors will continue to be considered a moral issue, or will people come to see their non-vital organs as "investments" to be sold in time of economic need? If they do, does the government have the right to prevent people from selling their organs? Why or why not? If an individual wants to sell an organ in order to make money, does a surgeon have the right and/or the responsibility to refuse to perform the operation? Write a composition explaining your opinions.

5 **Write in your journal.** Would you volunteer as a living organ donor? If so, under what circumstances would you do so? If not, why not?

Follow-up Activities

G

1. Refer to the **Self-Evaluation of Reading Strategies** on page 178. Check off the strategies you used to understand "Sales of Kidneys Prompt New Laws and Debate." Think about the strategies you didn't use, and apply them to help you understand the readings that follow.

2. Look at the graph carefully, and answer the related questions.

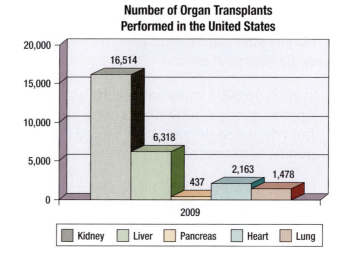

Number of Organ Transplants Performed in the United States

a. What does this graph show?

_____

_____

b. In 2009, what type of organ transplant was the least frequent?

_____

c. In 2009, what type of organ transplant was the most frequent?

_____

d. Based on what you read in the article, what is the reason this organ is transplanted most frequently?

_____

_____

_____

3 Look at the graph carefully, and answer the related questions.

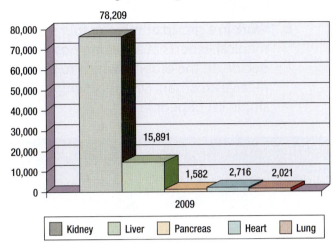

Waiting List for Organs in the United States

78,209

15,891

1,582   2,716   2,021

2009

Kidney   Liver   Pancreas   Heart   Lung

a. What does this graph show?

_____

_____

b. In 2009, which organ was the most needed for a transplant?

_____

c. In 2009, which organ was the least needed for a transplant?

_____

d. What conclusions might you draw from the information in *both* of these bar graphs?

_____

_____

_____

e. Review both graphs. Who seems to have the best chance for an organ transplant? Explain your answer.

_____

_____

_____

4 **a.** Below is a list of nine people who need heart transplants. Working alone, place these people in order of priority for a transplant. What factors (e.g. age, sex) should determine which patients receive priority?

b. Work in a group of three or four students. Your group is a panel of medical experts at a leading hospital in a large city. Your group must decide on the order in which to place these patients on the list to receive an organ. Discuss your individual decisions; then negotiate a single list of people in the order they will be placed on the waiting list.

Your Order	Your Group's Order	Sex	Age	Occupation	Personal Information	Length of Time Already Waiting
		F	36	housewife	3 children	12 months
		M	6	first grader	—	18 months
		M	71	heart surgeon	2 children, 3 grandchildren	9 months
		M	40	truck driver	widowed, 1 child	9 months
		F	24	kindergarten teacher	single, 2 siblings	12 months
		F	15	high school student	5 siblings	18 months
		F	47	cancer specialist	divorced, no children	12 months
		F	39	ESL teacher	married, 3 children	6 months
		M	52	banker	married, 1 child	10 months

UNIT 3   TECHNOLOGY AND ETHICAL ISSUES

Cloze Quiz

Complete the passage with words from the list. Use each word only once.

banning	hospitals	pick	sale
cadaver	impoverished	possible	supply
countries	kidneys	practice	traffic
dead	law	punishment	transplant
disclosed	organ	recipient	waiting

Last summer Colin Benton died after receiving a kidney

_____ at a private London hospital. Several months later,
(1)

however, his case made headlines throughout Britain when his widow

_____ that her husband's kidney transplant had come from
(2)

a Turkish citizen who was paid $3,300 to fly to Britain and donate the

_____ . Concern in Britain over issues raised in the case resulted
(3)

in a law passed on July 28,1989, in Parliament _____ the sale of
(4)

human organs for transplant.

But as Britain was moving to make the _____ of human
(5)

organs unlawful, as it is in the United States, ethicists and policy analysts

in the United States were beginning to suggest that paying donors, or their

estates, may be an effective way to increase the _____ of organs
(6)

available for transplant.

Doctors, lawyers and health authorities say the sale of organs by

_____ donors is a growing phenomenon. Because it is
(7)

_____ to live with just one kidney and because demand for the
(8)

organs is so high, _____ are among the most popular organs for
(9)

commercial transactions.

The new British _____ makes it a criminal offense
(10)
to give or receive money for supplying organs of either a living or

_____ person. It also prohibits acting as a broker in such an
(11)
arrangement, advertising for organs for payment or transplanting an organ
from a live donor not closely related to the _____ .
(12)

A new computerized nationwide registry, which records all transplants
from both live donors and cadavers, will be used to help enforce the law.
_____ for breaking the law is either a $3,300 fine or three
(13)
months in prison. Doctors convicted under the law could lose their right to
_____ medicine.
(14)

Britain has had a transplant law since the 1961 Human Tissue Act,
which deemed it unethical for a practitioner to _____ in
(15)
human organs. The British law applies only to transplants performed in
the nation's private _____ and not to those overseen by
(16)
the government-supported National Health Service, which provides free
medical care for British citizens. The service, which has not used paid donors,
gets first _____ of all kidneys available for transplant in the
(17)
nation. At present, about 1,600 transplants are performed each year, with a
_____ list of about 3,600 patients.
(18)

But, as in the United States, many patients from _____
(19)
without high-quality kidney care come to Britain each year to undergo
transplants in private hospitals. These hospitals rely on _____
(20)
kidneys or live donor transplants from relatives of patients.

9
CHAPTER

The Gift of Life: When One Body Can Save Another

Prereading Preparation

1 Read the title of the article and discuss it with a classmate. What do you think this reading will be about?

_____

_____

2 Read the following paragraphs about organ transplants. Work with a partner to answer the questions.

Paragraph One

A doctor's new dilemma: two weeks ago, Ronald Busuttil, director of UCLA's liver-transplant program, heard that a liver, just the right size and blood type, was suddenly available for a man who had been waiting for a transplant. The patient, severely ill but not on the verge of death, was being readied for the procedure when the phone rang. A five-year-old girl who had previously been given a transplant had suffered a catastrophe. Her liver had stopped functioning. Busuttil had to make a decision. "I had two desperately ill patients," he says, but the choice was clear. Without an immediate transplant, "the little girl certainly would have died."

a. What was the doctor's dilemma?

_____

_____

b. Describe each patient's condition:

The man's: _____

The little girl's: _____

c. What did the doctor decide to do?

_____

d. Do you agree with his decision? Why or why not?

_____

_____

Paragraph Two

In the world of advanced medical technology, the uses of living tissue have become very suddenly more complex and problematic. A newly born infant suffering from the fatal congenital malformation known as anencephaly will surely die within a few days of birth. Anencephaly means a partial or complete absence of the cerebrum, cerebellum and flat bones of the skull. Such babies could be an invaluable source for organs and tissues for other needy infants. Is that sort of "harvesting" all right?

a. Is an anencephalic infant healthy? Why or why not?

_____

b. What will happen to such an infant?

_____

c. What is the ethical dilemma in this case?

_____

_____

d. What is your opinion on this matter? In other words, **Is that sort of "harvesting" all right?**

_____

_____

_____

The Gift of Life: When One Body Can Save Another

by Lance Morrow, *Time*

1   Now the long quest was ending. A 14-month-old girl named Marissa Ayala lay anesthetized upon an operating table in the City of Hope National Medical Center in Duarte, California. A surgeon inserted a one-inch-long needle into the baby's hip and slowly began to draw marrow. In 20 minutes, they removed

5   about a cup of the viscous red liquid.

The medical team then rushed the marrow to a hospital room where Marissa's 19-year-old sister Anissa lay waiting. Through a Hickman catheter inserted in the chest, the doctor began feeding the baby's marrow into Anissa's veins. The marrow needed only to be dripped into the girl's bloodstream. There the healthy

10   marrow cells began to find their way to the bones.

Done. If all goes well, if rejection does not occur or a major infection set in, the marrow will do the work. It will give life to the older sister, who otherwise would have died of chronic myelogenous leukemia. Doctors rate the chance of success at 70%.

15   The Ayala family had launched itself upon a sequence of nervy, life-or-death adventures to arrive at the denouement last week. Anissa's leukemia was diagnosed three years ago. In such cases, the patient usually dies within five years unless she receives a marrow transplant. Abe and Mary Ayala, who own a speedometer-repair business, began a nationwide search for a donor whose

20   marrow would be a close match for Anissa's. The search, surrounded by much poignant publicity, failed.

The Ayalas did not passively accept their daughter's fate. They knew from their doctors that the best hope for Anissa lay in a marrow transplant from a sibling, but the marrow of her only brother, Airon, was incompatible. Her life,

25   it seemed, could depend on a sibling who did not yet exist.

First, Abe had to have his vasectomy surgically reversed, a procedure with a success rate of just 40%. That done, Mary Ayala ventured to become pregnant at the age of 43. The odds were one in four that the baby's bone marrow would match her sister's. In April 1990 Mary bore a daughter, Marissa. Fetal stem

30   cells were extracted from the umbilical cord and frozen for use along with the marrow in last week's transplant. Then everyone waited for the optimum moment—the baby had to grow old enough and strong enough to donate safely even while her older sister's time was waning.

Twelve days before the operation, Anissa began receiving intensive doses of radiation and chemotherapy to kill her diseased bone marrow. As a result, she is losing her hair. Her blood count is plummeting. Her immune system has gone out of business. But in two to four weeks, the new cells should take over and start their work of giving Anissa a new life.

The drama of the Ayalas—making the baby, against such long odds, to save the older daughter—seemed to many to be a miracle. To others, it was profoundly, if sometimes obscurely, troubling. What disturbed was the spectacle of a baby being brought in to the world . . . to serve as a means, a biological resupply vehicle. The baby did not consent to be used. The parents created the new life then used that life for their own purposes, however noble. Would the baby have agreed to the transplant if she had been able to make the choice?

People wanting a baby have many reasons—reasons frivolous, sentimental, practical, emotional, biological. Farm families need children to work the fields. In much of the world, children are social security for old age. They are vanity items for many people, an extension of ego. Or a sometimes desperate measure to try to save a marriage that is failing. Says Dr. Rudolf Brutoco, Marissa Ayala's pediatrician: "Does it make sense to conceive a child so that little Johnny can have a sister, while it is not acceptable to conceive the same child so that Johnny can live?" In American society, procreation is a personal matter. Crack addicts or convicted child abusers are free to have children.

Considered on the family's own terms, their behavior is hard to fault. The first duty of parents is to protect their children. The Ayalas say they never considered aborting the fetus if its marrow did not match Anissa's. They will cherish both daughters in the context of a miracle that allowed the older to live on and the younger to be born.

But their case resonated with meanings and dilemmas larger than itself. The case opened out upon a prospect of medical-technological possibility and danger. In the past it was mostly cadavers from which transplant organs were "harvested." Today, as with the Ayalas, life is being tapped to save life.[1]

Beyond the Ayala case, the ethics can become trickier. What if a couple conceives a baby in order to obtain matching marrow for another child; and what if amniocentesis shows that the tissue of the fetus is not compatible for transplant? Does the couple abort the fetus and then try again? Says Dr. Norman Fost, a pediatrician and ethicist at the University of Wisconsin: "If you believe that a woman is entitled to terminate a pregnancy for any reason at all, then it doesn't seem to me to make it any worse to terminate a pregnancy for this reason." But abortions are normally performed to end accidental pregnancies.

[1] Postscript: The transplant operation was successful. Anissa survived and Marissa suffered no adverse effects from the procedure.

What is the morality of ending a pregnancy that was very deliberately undertaken in the first place?

Transplant technology is developing so rapidly that new practices are outpacing society's ability to explore their moral implications. The first kidney transplants were performed over 35 years ago and were greeted as the brave new world: an amazing novelty. Today the transplant is part of the culture—conceptually dazzling, familiar in a weird way but morally unassimilated. The number of organ transplants exceeds 15,000 a year and is growing at an annual clip of 15%. The variety of procedures is also expanding as surgeons experiment with transplanting parts of the pancreas, the lung and other organs. As of last week, 23,276 people were on the waiting list of the United Network for Organ Sharing, a national registry and tracking service.

A dire shortage of organs for these patients helps make the world of transplants an inherently bizarre one. Seat-belt and motorcycle-helmet laws are bad news for those waiting for a donor. The laws reduce fatalities and therefore reduce available cadavers.

Most organs come from cadavers, but the number of living donors is rising. There were 1,778 last year, up 15% from 1989. Of these, 1,773 provided kidneys, nine provided portions of livers. Six of the living donors gave their hearts away. How? They were patients who needed heart-lung transplant packages. To make way for the new heart, they gave up the old one; doctors call it the "domino practice."

In 1972 Dr. Thomas Starzl, the renowned Pittsburgh surgeon who pioneered liver transplants, stopped performing live-donor transplants of any kind. He explained why in a speech in 1987: "The death of a single well-motivated and completely healthy living donor almost stops the clock worldwide. The most compelling argument against living donation is that it is not completely safe for the donor." Starzl said he knew of 20 donors who had died, though other doctors regard this number as miraculously low, since there have been more than 100,000 live-donor transplants.

There will never be enough cadaver organs to fill the growing needs of people dying from organ or tissue failure. This places higher and higher importance, and risk, on living relatives who might serve as donors. Organs that are either redundant (one of a pair of kidneys) or regenerative (bone marrow) become more and more attractive. Transplants become a matter of high-stakes risk calculation for the donor as well as the recipient and the intense emotions involved sometimes have people playing long shots.

Federal law now prohibits any compensation for organs in the United States. In China and India, there is a brisk trade in such organs as kidneys. Will the day come when Americans have a similar marketplace for organs? Turning the body into a commodity might in fact make families less willing to donate organs.

Reading Overview: Main Idea, Details, and Summary

Read the passage again. As you read, underline what you think are the most important ideas. Then, in one or two sentences, write the main idea of the reading. **Use your own words.**

Main Idea

_____

_____

_____

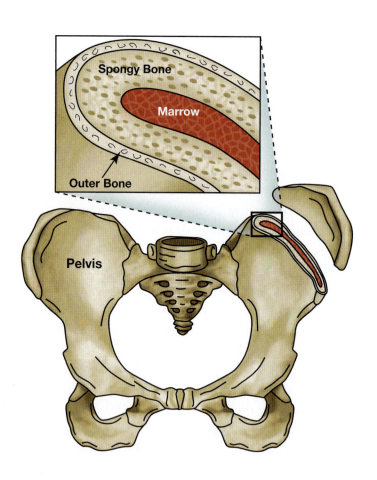

Details

Use the flowchart below to organize the information in the reading. Refer back to the information you underlined in the passage as a guide. When you have finished, write a brief summary of the reading. **Use your own words.**

THE GIFT OF LIFE: WHEN ONE BODY CAN SAVE ANOTHER

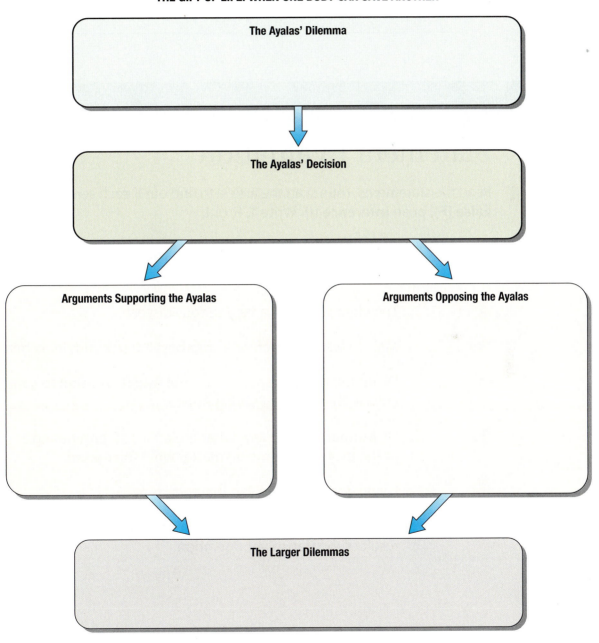

The Ayalas' Dilemma

The Ayalas' Decision

Arguments Supporting the Ayalas

Arguments Opposing the Ayalas

The Larger Dilemmas

Summary

_____

_____

_____

_____

_____

B Statement Evaluation

Read the statements. Then scan the article to find out if each sentence is **True (T)**, **False (F),** or an **Inference (I).** Write **T, F,** or **I.**

1 _____ The bone marrow was taken from 19-year-old Anissa and given to 14-month-old Marissa.

2 _____ The older sister has a very serious disease.

3 _____ Marissa was born before Anissa became sick with leukemia.

4 _____ Dr. Rudolf Brutoco agreed with the Ayalas' decision to conceive a child in the hopes of saving Anissa.

5 _____ Dr. Norman Fost believes that the ethics of terminating a pregnancy is the same no matter what the reason.

6 _____ Living donors have given their hearts away.

7 _____ Dr. Thomas Starzl worries that an organ recipient may die as a result of the transplant operation.

Reading Analysis

Read each question carefully. Circle the letter or number of the correct answer, or write the answer.

1 Read lines 7–8. A **catheter** is

   a. a type of medicine
   b. a thin plastic tube
   c. a small hole

2 Read lines 11–12. **If all goes well** means

   a. if the procedure works correctly
   b. if the sister dies
   c. if rejection occurs

3 Read lines 15–18.

   a. **Denouement** means

     1. problem
     2. solution
     3. hospital

   b. What does **in such cases** refer to?

_____

4 Read lines 22–25.

   a. What was **their daughter's fate?**

     1. She would be sick for a long time.
     2. She would die within five years.
     3. She would receive marrow from a stranger.

   b. **The marrow of her only brother . . . was incompatible** means

     1. the marrow of Airon and Anissa was the same
     2. the marrow of Airon and Anissa was different

   c. **A sibling who did not yet exist** refers to a sibling who

     1. has not been conceived yet
     2. has already been born
     3. is not yet old enough

5 Read lines 31–33.

    a. When is the **optimum moment?**

    _____

    b. Optimum means

        1. best
        2. worst
        3. after one year

6 Read lines 39–45. In this paragraph, what word is a synonym of **consent?**

_____

7 Read lines 53–54. What is **procreation?**

    a. Having children
    b. Taking drugs
    c. Making a choice

8 Read lines 68–71. To have an **abortion** means to

    a. become pregnant
    b. terminate a pregnancy
    c. continue a pregnancy

9 Read lines 85–87.

    a. What are **seat-belt and motorcycle-helmet laws?**

    _____

    b. Why are these laws **bad news for those waiting for a donor?**

    _____

    _____

10 Read lines 95–98.

    a. The death of a . . . completely healthy living donor almost stops the clock worldwide means that the death of a healthy living donor

        1. discourages other healthy people from donating an organ
        2. discourages doctors from performing transplant operations using healthy living donors
        3. both 1 and 2

    b. **Compelling** means

        1. convincing

        2. healthy

        3. interesting

11 Read line 108. **Prohibits any compensation** means

    a. you cannot receive money for donating an organ

    b. you cannot donate an organ from a cadaver

    c. you cannot donate an organ from a living donor

D Dictionary Skills

Read the excerpts from the article. Then read the dictionary entry for the boldfaced word and write the number of the definition that is appropriate for the context. Be prepared to explain your choice.

1 There will never be enough cadaver organs to fill the growing needs of people dying from organ or tissue **failure.**

    failure: _____

> **failure** **1** **a :** omission of occurrence or performance; *specifically* : a failing to perform a duty or expected action <failure to pay the rent on time> **b** (1) : a state of inability to perform a normal function <kidney failure> — compare HEART FAILURE (2) : an abrupt cessation of normal functioning <a power failure> **c** : a fracturing or giving way under stress <structural failure> **2** **a :** lack of success **b** : a failing in business : BANKRUPTCY **3** **a :** a falling short : DEFICIENCY <a crop failure> **b** : DETERIORATION, DECAY . . .

2 Considered on the family's own terms, the Ayalas' behavior (conceiving a baby to save their daughter) is hard to **fault.**

    fault: _____

> **fault** *intransitive verb* **1** : to commit a fault : ERR **2** : to fracture so as to produce a geologic fault
> *transitive verb* **1** : to find a fault in <easy to praise this book and to fault it—H. G. Roepke> **2** : to produce a geologic fault in . . .

By permission. From *Merriam-Webster's Collegiate® Dictionary,* 11th Edition © 2010 by Merriam-Webster, Incorporated (www.Merriam-Webster.com).

3 In 1972 Dr. Thomas Starzl, the renowned Pittsburgh surgeon who **pioneered** liver transplants, stopped performing live-donor transplants of any kind.

pioneer: _____

---

pioneer *intransitive verb* **1** : to act as a pioneer <pioneer*ed* in the development of airplanes>
transitive verb **1** : to open or prepare for others to follow; *also* : SETTLE **2** : to originate or take part in the development of

---

4 The drama of the Ayalas—making the baby, against such long odds, to save the older daughter—seemed to many to be a miracle. To others, it was **profoundly,** if sometimes obscurely, troubling.

profound: _____

---

profound **1** **a** : having intellectual depth and insight **b** : difficult to fathom or understand **2** **a** : extending far below the surface **b** : coming from, reaching to, or situated at a depth : DEEP-SEATED <a profound sigh> **3** **a** : characterized by intensity of feeling or quality **b** : all encompassing : COMPLETE <profound sleep> <profound deafness>

Word Partnership	Use *failure* with:
adj.	**afraid of** failure, **doomed to** failure, **complete** failure, **dismal** failure
n.	**feelings of** failure, **risk of** failure, **success or** failure, **engine** failure, **heart** failure, **kidney** failure, **liver** failure, **business** failure
v.	failure **to communicate**

Word Partnership	Use *fault* with:
prep.	**at** fault, **to a** fault
adj.	**generous to a** fault
v.	**find** fault

Critical Thinking Strategies

Read each question carefully, and write a response. Remember that there is no one correct answer. Your response depends on what **you** think.

1 What do you think is Dr. Rudolf Brutoco's opinion of the Ayalas' decision to have another child in the hopes of saving their daughter's life?

_____

_____

2 a. Why did Dr. Starzl stop performing live-donor transplants of any kind?

_____

_____

b. Why do other doctors regard the number of donors who have died as **miraculously low?**

_____

_____

3 Why will there be a **higher and higher importance, and risk** for living relatives who may become donors?

_____

_____

Another Perspective

Read the article and answer the questions that follow.

CD 2
Track 06

Saving Her Sister's Life

Teen Vogue

1   *In 1990, Marissa Ayala's birth stirred a national debate—should families conceive one child to save another's life? In her own words, 18-year-old Marissa shares her story.*

My sister, Anissa, is like my second mom. Even though she's 18 years older than
5   me, I don't know how much closer you could be with someone. In 1988, when she was 16, Anissa was diagnosed with leukemia. If she didn't find a bone marrow donor, doctors said, she would die within three to five years. My parents weren't matches, so for a few years they went through every organization they could—the Life-Savers Foundation of America, the National Marrow Donor Program, City of
10 Hope—to find donors. They couldn't find a single match. At the time, the Hispanic rating for the National Marrow Donor Program was practically nonexistent, which means there were hardly any Hispanics on the list as donors. Since that's our heritage, it wasn't likely my parents would find someone who could work as a match for my sister.

15 Because matches are more common within families than with nonrelatives, every single extended family member got tested, but none of them matched with Anissa. Finally, one of my mom's best friends said as a joke, "Mary, you should have another baby." My mom, who was 43 at the time, thought her friend was crazy. But one night my mom dreamed that God was telling her to have a baby.
20 She took that as a sign, and in April 1990 I was born. My parents were hoping I would be a match.

When I was old enough to be tested, I turned out to be a perfect match for my sister. My family was really excited and had me donate bone marrow to her 14 months after I was born—my marrow was transplanted into hers to stimulate
25 healthy blood-cell growth. It was a total success. I recovered perfectly—my parents even have a video of me running around the same day I had my surgery. Although at first my sister had to be in an isolation room for a while so that no germs could get to her, she recovered well. She's been cancer-free for the past 18 years.

30　　There has always been a lot of media attention surrounding our family because
of our situation, though. It was apparently really controversial that my parents were
having a baby just to save their other daughter's life. I don't remember a lot of that,
because I was so much younger. When I was a baby, Anissa and I were on the cover
of *Time* and there was a made-for-TV movie on NBC in 1993 called *For the Love of*
35　*My Child: The Anissa Ayala Story,* made about my family's experience.

　　I first started really researching my own story when I was in the seventh grade.
My friends were Googling themselves and nothing came up, but when I searched
for myself a lot of news articles popped up. I read negative comments from a few
newspapers about how my parents were just using me to save my sister's life and
40　weren't going to love me, and that what they did was morally wrong. It surprised
me. I thought, "Really? People think about my family like that?" Some of the articles
said that if I hadn't been a perfect match for my sister, my parents would have
disowned me. And that just wasn't the case.

　　I try to see both sides of the story, but I ultimately don't agree with the critics.
45　They were probably just looking out for my safety, thinking that my parents were
going to have a baby solely for the purpose of saving their child. But they don't
know us personally: My family loves me so much.

　　Every year our family takes part in the Relay for Life cancer walk and we raise
money for the American Cancer Society. We try to spread the message that the need
50　for marrow donors is great. And more important, that despite being diagnosed with
whatever type of cancer, there's a way to get through it.

　　There are so many ways growing up as "the baby who saved her sister" has
influenced my life. I've taken it, been humbled by it, and have grown from it. But it
won't be my whole life story. In the future, I plan to study either child development
55　or psychology. My dad always tells me, "Marissa, you should do something you want
to do every day." I want to help people.

1　a. Marissa says, **There has always been a lot of media attention
surrounding our family because of our situation.** Why was there a lot
of media attention?

_____

_____

_____

b. Give some examples of the media attention.

_____

_____

2 **a.** What negative comments did the critics make about the Ayala family?

_____

_____

b. Does Marissa agree with them? Why or why not?

_____

3 Many people know Marissa Ayala as **the baby who saved her sister.** How has this influenced her life today? How will this influence her in the future?

_____

_____

_____

4 Compare the articles, "The Gift of Life" and "Saving Her Sister's Life." How are they different? How are they similar?

_____

_____

_____

_____

_____

Topics for Discussion and Writing

1 In a magazine survey, 47% of American people said they believe it is acceptable for parents to conceive a child in order to provide an organ or tissue that will save the life of another one of their children. However, 37% of Americans believe this is unacceptable. What do you think? Write a letter to the magazine explaining your position. Be sure to make your reasons clear.

2 What do you think is the general opinion on living-to-living organ donation (for example, the donation of a kidney or a lung lobe) in your country? Is this practice legal? Write a paragraph about living-to-living organ donation in your country. Compare it with your classmates' descriptions of living-to-living organ donation in their countries. How are the policies similar in various countries? How are they different?

3 **Write in your journal.** What is your opinion about the Ayala case? Do you approve of their decision to have another child in order to save their older daughter? Explain your opinion.

Follow-up Activities

1 Refer to the **Self-Evaluation of Reading Strategies** on the next page. Check off the strategies you used to understand "The Gift of Life." Evaluate your strategy use over the first nine chapters. Which strategies have you begun to use that you didn't use before? Which strategies do you use consistently? Which strategies have you added to the list? Which strategies are becoming automatic? To what extent have you applied these strategies to other reading you do?

Self-Evaluation of Reading Strategies			
Strategies	Readings		
	"Matters of Life and Death"	"Sales of Kidneys"	"The Gift of Life"
I read the title and try to predict what the reading will be about.			
I use my knowledge of the world to help me understand the text.			
I read as though I *expect* the text to have meaning.			
I use illustrations to help me understand the text.			
I ask myself questions about the text.			
I use a variety of types of context clues.			
I take chances in order to identify meaning.			
I continue if I am not successful.			
I identify and underline main ideas.			
I connect details with main ideas.			
I summarize the reading in my own words.			
I skip unnecessary words.			
I look up words correctly in the dictionary.			
I connect the reading to other material I have read.			
I do not translate into my native language.			

2 Conduct an in-class survey using the questions in the following chart. Record the responses in the chart. (You may use your data later if you decide to do an out-of-class survey on the same questions.) Discuss the responses in class.

Questions	Yes	No
1. Is it morally acceptable for parents to conceive a child in order to provide an organ or tissue that will save the life of another one of their children?		
2. Is it morally acceptable to remove a kidney or other nonessential organ from a living person for use in another person's body?		
3. Would you donate a kidney for transplant to a close relative who needed it?		
4. Is it ethical to ask a child under the age of 18 to give up a kidney for a transplant to a relative?		
5. If you or a close relative had a fatal disease that could possibly be cured by a transplant, which of these would you be willing to do?		
a. Purchase the necessary organ or tissue		
b. Conceive a child to provide the necessary organ or tissue		
c. Take legal action to force a relative to donate		

Cloze Quiz

Complete the passage with words from the list. Use each word only once.

consent	frivolous	optimum	sibling
denouement	incompatible	pregnant	success
disturbed	launched	radiation	surgeon
donor	life	rejection	transplant
failed	marrow	safely	unless

A 14-month-old girl named Marissa Ayala lay anesthetized upon an operating table in the City of Hope National Medical Center. A _____ (1) inserted a one-inch-long needle into the baby's hip and slowly began to draw marrow.

The medical team then rushed the _____ (2) to a hospital room where Marissa's 19-year-old sister Anissa lay waiting. The doctor fed the baby's marrow into Anissa's veins. There the healthy marrow cells began to find their way to the bones.

Done. If all goes well, if _____ (3) does not occur or a major infection set in, the marrow will do the work. It will give life to the older sister, who otherwise would have died of leukemia. Doctors rate the chance of success at 70%.

The Ayala family had _____ (4) itself upon a sequence of nervy, life-or-death adventures to arrive at the _____ (5) last week. Anissa's leukemia was diagnosed three years ago. In such cases, the patient usually dies within five years _____ (6) she receives a marrow transplant. Abe and Mary Ayala began a nationwide search for a _____ (7) whose marrow would be a close match for Anissa's. The search _____ (8) .

The Ayalas did not passively accept their daughter's fate. They knew from their doctors that the best hope for Anissa lay in a marrow transplant from a _____ (9) , but the marrow of her only brother, Airon, was _____ (10) . Her life, it seemed, could depend on a sibling who did not yet exist.

First, Abe had to have his vasectomy surgically reversed, a procedure with a _____ (11) rate of just 40%. That done, Mary Ayala ventured to become _____ (12) at the age of 43. In April 1990 Mary bore a daughter, Marissa. Then everyone waited for the _____ (13) moment—the baby had to grow old enough and strong enough to donate _____ (14) , even while her older sister's time was waning.

Twelve days before the operation, Anissa began receiving intensive doses of _____ (15) and chemotherapy to kill her diseased bone marrow. But in two to four weeks, the new cells should take over and start their work of giving Anissa a new life.

The drama of the Ayalas—making the baby, against such long odds, to save the older daughter—seemed to many to be a miracle. To others, it was profoundly, if sometimes obscurely, troubling. What _____ (16) was the spectacle of a baby being brought in to the world . . . to serve as a means, a biological resupply vehicle. The baby did not _____ (17) to be used. The parents created the new _____ (18) then used that life for their own purposes, however noble. Would the baby have agreed to the _____ (19) if she had been able to make the choice?

People wanting a baby have many reasons—reasons _____ (20) , sentimental, practical, emotional, biological. Farm families need children to work the fields. In much of the world, children are social security for old age. They are vanity items for many people, an extension of ego.

Crossword Puzzle

Read the clues on the next page. Write the answers in the correct spaces in the puzzle.

Crossword Puzzle Clues

ACROSS CLUES

2. This paragraph is part of a longer reading. It is an _____ from a reading.
6. The past tense of **put**
7. An electronic device that controls the heartbeat
10. The _____ time to do something is the best time to do it.
14. Deadly; terminal
17. Topics such as capital punishment, euthanasia, and assisted suicide are very _____ .
18. Kidneys, heart, lungs, pancreas, liver
20. The solution to a problem or a difficult situation is its _____ .
22. Very poor
23. A _____ is a person who sacrifices himself for a cause or for another person.
25. Looking in _____ means looking back at a past event.
26. Make known; reveal

DOWN CLUES

1. The opposite of **down**
3. A thin plastic tube used in medical procedures
4. When we _____ something to be right or wrong, we judge it to be right or wrong.
5. Minor; trivial
8. Necessary
9. A person who gives something voluntarily is a _____ .
11. The center part of bone
12. Keep in an existing state
13. A dead body; a corpse
15. A subject of investigation
16. Reflex; involuntary
19. Direct one's efforts or attention to
21. A code of _____ is a system of moral values.
24. **I, me; we, _____**

The Environment

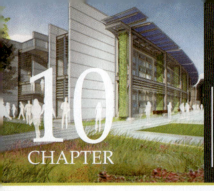

10 CHAPTER

Students Dig into Sustainable Farming at Vermont College

Prereading Preparation

1 Read the title of the article and look at the photograph below.

a. What do you think the students are learning at this college?

_____

_____

b. What is **sustainable farming?** If you're not sure, read the definition in the footnote on the bottom of page 187. Is sustainable farming important? Why or why not?

_____

_____

_____

c. Where is this farm?

_____

d. What kind of animal is in the photo? What are these animals used for?

_____

_____

CD 2
Track 07

Students Dig into Sustainable Farming at Vermont College

by Lisa Rathke, _The Associated Press_

1 Devin Lyons typically starts his days this summer cooking breakfast with fresh eggs from the farm's chicken coop. Then, depending on the weather, he and a dozen other college students might cut hay in the field using a team of oxen, turn compost, or weed vegetable beds.

5 While other college students are in stuffy classrooms, about a dozen are earning credit tending a Vermont farm. For 13 weeks, 12 credits and about $12,500, the Green Mountain College students plow fields with oxen or horses, milk cows, weed crops, and grow and make their own food, part of an intensive course in sustainable agriculture using the least amount of fossil fuels. "Lots of

10 schools study sustainable agriculture[1], but I don't think any of them put it into practice," said spokesman Kevin Coburn.

There are no tractors on the 22 acres next to the brick campus of the small liberal arts college on the edge of the town—just two teams of oxen, and goats, pigs, two cows, and chickens. Students sleep in tents on the field's edge, next to a

15 river. They spend about six hours a week in classes in the old farmhouse, learning theory on organic crop and animal management; management of farm systems; development of agricultural technologies with a focus on human and animal power; and the social and cultural importance of regional food. The rest of the time they're out in the field, or doing homework and working on research projects.

20 "So they're actually seeing the applications firsthand," said Kenneth Mulder, manager of the college's Cerridwen Farm, who runs the summer program.

College farming is growing. According to the Rodale Institute in Pennsylvania, more than 80 schools now have hands-on and classroom-based

---

[1] Environmentally friendly methods of farming that allow the production of crops or livestock without damage to the farm as an ecosystem, including effects on soil and water supplies

farm programs. Many of them are organic vegetable farms, but students don't necessarily earn as many credits as Green Mountain College students do, nor do they get to work with teams of oxen. Sterling College, also in Vermont, has a similar program. "It's traditionally been one of the leaders in environmental studies and it is because they put their studies where their mouth is in really getting students out and doing and practicing the sort of environmentally enlightened work that some talk about in class," said Roland King, a spokesman for the National Association of Independent Colleges and Universities.

For her research project, Cassie Callahan, 18, Conway, N.H., wants to water plants with gray water collected from the farm's solar shower, attached to the greenhouse. But she's not sure yet if the soap—even biodegradable soap—will harm the plants if it's not diluted. Her real love is working with draft horses. She jumps at the chance every time and even has a new tattoo of a team of horses on her shin. In her hometown, she had a job driving horse-drawn sleighs and wagons and now has learned the animals can be used for more than tourism. She hopes to be a farmer, supporting herself and selling a little on the side. "You know, people have jobs to make money to feed themselves and clothe themselves but I'd much rather have my job be to feed and clothe myself," she said.

Green Mountain College hopes to turn out farmers and has several alumni running farms nearby. Other students are interested in food-related fields— whether it's organizing nonprofits, working on policy or overseas development work. Lyons, 19, doesn't know if he'll farm but so far he's learned a lot. Growing up in suburban Jefferson, N.J., he said he didn't know much about where his food came from and was never exposed to organic farms. "I never really got the connection between the cooked chicken on my plate—and it was a dead chicken that was killed—I just never really thought about it," he said.

UNIT 4   THE ENVIRONMENT

Reading Overview: Main Idea, Details, and Summary

Read the passage again. As you read, underline what you think are the most important ideas. Then, in one or two sentences, write the main idea of the reading. **Use your own words.**

Main Idea

_____

_____

_____

Details

Use the outline below to organize the information in the reading. Refer back to the information you underlined in the passage as a guide. When you have finished, write a brief summary of the reading. **Use your own words.**

Sustainable Farming Program at Green Mountain College	
Location of Program:	
Length of Program:	
Cost of Program:	
Number of Credits:	
Types of Classes:	
Types of Field Work:	
Example of Research Project:	
Purpose of the Program:	
Differences between Green Mountain College and Other Farm Programs:	

Summary

_____

_____

_____

_____

_____

B

Statement Evaluation

Read the statements. Then scan the article to find out if each sentence is **True (T), False (F),** or an **Inference (I).** Write **T, F,** or **I.**

1 _____ Devin Lyons is earning college credits by working on a farm.

2 _____ Students at Green Mountain College take classes in addition to working in the fields.

3 _____ Students in the 13-week farming program at Green Mountain College live on the farm.

4 _____ All students in college farming programs earn the same number of credits as the students at Green Mountain College earn.

5 _____ Cassie Callahan believes that some biodegradable soap may be harmful to plants.

6 _____ All the students in the sustainable farming program want to become farmers.

7 _____ Some former students of Green Mountain College have their own farms now.

Reading Analysis

Read each question carefully. Circle the letter or number of the correct answer, or write the answer.

1 Read lines 1–2. A **chicken coop** is
   a. a refrigerator for chicken eggs
   b. a small building for chickens
   c. a food store on a farm

2 Read lines 5–11. According to the author, which is preferable for college students studying farming?
   a. Sitting in a stuffy classroom
   b. Being outside doing farm work

3 Read lines 12–14. What do the students use instead of tractors on the 22 acres?

   _____

4 Read lines 15–21. How are the students seeing applications **firsthand?**
   a. By learning about them in class
   b. By watching their teachers perform them
   c. By doing them themselves

5 Read lines 22–24. Learning farming techniques on a college campus
   a. is becoming more common
   b. is becoming less common

6 Read lines 27–31. **They put their studies where their mouth is** means
   a. they talk a lot about environmental studies in the classroom
   b. they eat the food that they grow at the college
   c. they actually put into practice what they teach

7 Read lines 32–34. **Gray water** is
   a. very dirty
   b. a little dirty
   c. clean, but not clear

8 Read lines 34–35. **Biodegradable** means that something
   a. is capable of naturally breaking down into harmless materials
   b. is capable of cleaning objects if diluted
   c. is capable of harming plants if applied directly to them

9 Read line 35. **Draft horses** are

　　a. fast, and used for racing
　　b. beautiful, and used in shows
　　c. strong, and used for work

10 Read lines 45–47. Before he attended Green Mountain College, Devin Lyons

　　a. had never seen a real chicken living on a farm
　　b. had never realized that the chicken he ate had been a living animal
　　c. had never killed a chicken in order to eat it

Dictionary Skills

Read the excerpts from the article. Then read the dictionary entry for the boldfaced word and write the number of the definition that is appropriate for the context. Be prepared to explain your choice.

1 Then, depending on the weather, he and a dozen other college students might cut hay in the field using a team of oxen, turn compost, or weed vegetable **beds.**

　　bed: _____

> **bed** **1** **a :** a piece of furniture on or in which to lie and sleep **b** (1) : a place of sex relations (2) : marital relationship (3) : close association : CAHOOTS <a legislator in bed with lobbyists> **c :** a place for sleeping **d :** SLEEP; *also :* a time for sleeping <took a walk before bed> **e** (1) : a mattress filled with soft material (2) : BEDSTEAD **f :** the equipment and services needed to care for one hospitalized patient or hotel guest **2** : a flat or level surface : as **a :** a plot of ground prepared for plants; *also :* the plants grown in such a plot **b :** the bottom of a body of water; *especially :* an area of sea bottom supporting a heavy growth of a particular organism <an oyster bed> **3** : a supporting surface or structure : FOUNDATION . . .

2 While other college students are in stuffy classrooms, about a dozen are earning credit **tending** a Vermont farm.

　　tend: _____

> **tend** *intransitive verb* **1** *archaic* : LISTEN **2** : to pay attention : apply oneself <tend to your own affairs> <tend to our correspondence> **3** : to act as an attendant : SERVE <tend*ed* to his wife> **4** *obsolete* : AWAIT
> *transitive verb* **1** *archaic* : to attend as a servant **2 a** : to apply oneself to the care of : watch over <tend*ed* her sick father> **b** : to have or take charge of as a caretaker or overseer <tend the sheep> **c** : CULTIVATE, FOSTER **d** : to manage the operations of : MIND <tend the store> <tend the fire>

3 They spend about six hours a week in classes in the old farmhouse, learning theory on **organic** crop and animal management.

organic: _____

> **organic** **1** *archaic* : INSTRUMENTAL **2 a** : of, relating to, or arising in a bodily organ **b** : affecting the structure of the organism **3 a** (1) : of, relating to, or derived from living organisms <organic evolution> (2) : of, relating to, yielding, or involving the use of food produced with the use of feed or fertilizer of plant or animal origin without employment of chemically formulated fertilizers, growth stimulants, antibiotics, or pesticides <organic farming> <organic produce> **b** (1) : of, relating to, or containing carbon compounds (2) : relating to, being, or dealt with by a branch of chemistry concerned with the carbon compounds of living beings and most other carbon compounds . . .

4 "They're actually seeing the **applications** firsthand."

application: _____

> **application** **1** : an act of applying : **a** (1) : an act of putting to use <application of new techniques> (2) : a use to which something is put <new applications for old remedies> (3) : a program (as a word processor or a spreadsheet) that performs one of the major tasks for which a computer is used **b** : an act of administering or superposing <application of paint to a house> **c** : assiduous attention <succeeds by application to her studies> **2 a** : REQUEST, PETITION <an application for financial aid> **b** : a form used in making a request **3** : the practical inference to be derived from a discourse (as a moral tale) . . .

Word Partnership	Use *application* with:
n.	**college** application, application **form**, **grant/loan** application, **job** application, **membership** application, application **software**
adj.	**practical** application
v.	**accept/reject an** application, **file/submit an** application, **fill out an** application

By permission. From Merriam-Webster's Collegiate® Dictionary, 11th Edition © 2010 by Merriam-Webster, Incorporated (www.Merriam-Webster.com).

Critical Thinking Strategies

Read each question carefully, and write a response. Remember that there is no one correct answer. Your response depends on what **you** think.

1 There are no tractors on Green Mountain College's Cerridwen Farm. Why not? Why do the students use oxen and draft horses instead of tractors?

_____

_____

_____

2 Classroom-based farm programs, such as the one at Green Mountain College, are becoming more common in the U.S. today. What do you think are reasons for this?

_____

_____

_____

3 In some colleges, students study agriculture, but do not actually do farm work as part of their coursework. What might be some advantages and disadvantages of classroom learning versus hands-on learning?

_____

_____

_____

4 Organically grown food tends to be more expensive than food grown using chemical fertilizers and insecticides.

a. What are the advantages and disadvantages of growing food organically?

_____

_____

b. What are the advantages and disadvantages of growing food using chemicals?

_____

_____

Another Perspective

Read the article and answer the questions that follow.

CD 2
Track 08

NASA Goes Green with New Sustainability Base

by Clara Moskowitz, *SPACE.com*

1   One of NASA's most ambitious new projects isn't in space, but on the ground. The agency is planning to build its most environmentally-friendly building at its Ames Research Center in Moffett Field, Calif. The structure, to be called Sustainability Base, will likely be the "greenest" building in the federal
5   government, said Steve Zornetzer, Associate Center Director at NASA Ames. The ceremonial groundbreaking on the $20.6 million building is set for August 25, and construction is expected to be complete in the near future.

Utilizing solar panels, fuel cells, water recycling systems, and even technology derived from NASA's human and robotic space exploration missions, the
10   building will aim for a LEED (Leadership in Energy and Environmental Design) platinum plus certification. Sustainability Base is designed to consume no net energy—in other words, it will power itself. And compared to conventional buildings of equal size, it will use 90 percent less potable water.

"I decided that if we're going to build an energy efficient building, why don't
15   we build the most energy efficient building we can possibly build, in the spirit of what we need to do for this country," Zornetzer told SPACE.com.

The centerpiece of the building's cutting-edge technology is its intelligent control system, which is based on ones originally developed for NASA spacecraft. A computer inside Sustainability Base will connect to the Internet to call up weather forecasts for the local area to help it plan environmental control. It will have access to electronic calendars of workers in the building, so it can predict how many people will be at a given meeting, and adjust heating and cooling systems appropriately.

Instead of air conditioning, Sustainability Base is designed to cool itself from geothermal wells that route naturally cooled water from underneath the ground through pipes and cooling panels inside the building. The computer will also control the windows, so when a chill nighttime breeze flows near, the building can take advantage of it too.

NASA also plans to encourage occupants to try to improve their own levels of energy efficiency, which the building will keep track of and report to people on their laptops. "We want people in the building to compete, to try to optimize their own energy efficiency so they can get the greatest amount of work done with the least amount of watts," Zornetzer said.

Sustainability Base will serve mainly as an office building, but may also house some scientific research and engineering. The cost of the building will be provided by a NASA program called Renovation by Replacement, which aims to replace antiquated facilities with more modern, energy efficient ones. The building was designed by the AECOM and William McDonough + Partners architectural firms. Swinerton Inc. will carry out the construction.

Proposed NASA Sustainability Base

1 How will the NASA Sustainability Base be **green?**

_____

_____

2 **a.** What is the purpose of the **intelligence control system?**

_____

b. What will it do?

_____

_____

3 How can the occupants of the NASA Sustainability Base help conserve energy?

_____

4 What will this building be used for?

_____

_____

G

Topics for Discussion and Writing

1 Sustainable farming is important to the environment. What are some things you can do everyday to help the environment? Make a list, and then compare your list with your classmates' lists.

2 What do you think is the biggest threat to our environment, e.g. air pollution, overpopulation, etc.? Why is this dangerous to our lives? Support your opinion with examples.

3 **Write in your journal.** Do you think that students should receive college credits for studying sustainable farming? Why or why not?

Follow-up Activities

1. Refer to the **Self-Evaluation of Reading Strategies** on page 240. Check off the strategies you used to understand "Students Dig into Sustainable Farming at Vermont College." Think about the strategies you didn't use, and apply them to understand the readings that follow.

2. Read the description of the introductory course in the Sustainable Agriculture Program at Central Carolina Community College of North Carolina. Then work with a partner. How can sustainable farming benefit the economy, the environment, and society? In other words, why is sustainable agriculture good for the economy, the environment, and society? Write your ideas in the flow chart.

AGR 139 Introduction to Sustainable Agriculture

This course will provide students with a clear perspective on the principles, history and practices of sustainable agriculture in our local and global communities. Students will be introduced to the economic, environmental and social impacts of agriculture. Upon completion, students should be able to identify the principles of sustainable agriculture as they relate to basic production practices.

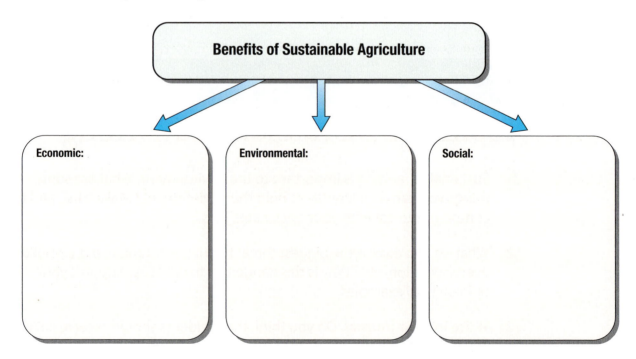

Benefits of Sustainable Agriculture

Economic:

Environmental:

Social:

Cloze Quiz

Complete the passage with words from the list. Use each word only once.

acres	course	homework	sleep
amount	credit	oxen	students
breakfast	fields	practice	sustainable
college	firsthand	rest	theory
coop	food	river	weather

Devin Lyons typically starts his days this summer cooking

_____ with fresh eggs from the farm's chicken
(1)

_____ . Then, depending on the _____ , he
(2)   (3)

and a dozen other college students might cut hay in the field using a team of

_____ , turn compost or weed vegetable beds.
(4)

While other college _____ are in stuffy classrooms,
(5)

about a dozen are earning _____ tending a Vermont farm.
(6)

For 13 weeks, 12 credits and about $12,500, the Green Mountain College

students plow _____ with oxen or horses, milk cows,
(7)

weed crops and grow and make their own _____ , part
(8)

of an intensive _____ in sustainable agriculture using
(9)

the least _____ of fossil fuels. "Lots of schools study
(10)

_____ agriculture but I don't think any of them put it into
(11)

_____ ," said spokesman Kevin Coburn.
(12)

There are no tractors on the 22 _____ next to the brick
(13)

campus of the small liberal arts _____ on the edge of the
(14)

town—just two teams of oxen, and goats, pigs, two cows, and chickens. Students _____ in tents on the field's edge, next to a
(15)
_____ . They spend about six hours a week in classes in the
(16)
old farmhouse, learning _____ on organic crop and animal
(17)
management. The _____ of the time they're out in the field,
(18)
or doing _____ and working on research projects. "So they're
(19)
actually seeing the applications _____ ," said Kenneth Mulder,
(20)
manager of the college's Cerridwen Farm, who runs the summer program.

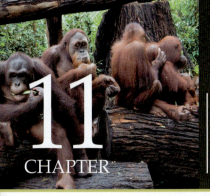

Wilder Places
for Wild Things

Prereading Preparation

1 Work with one or two partners. What do you know about traditional zoos? What do you know about modern zoos? Complete the chart.

Traditional Zoos	Modern Zoos

2 Why do you think zoos have changed in these ways?

_____

_____

_____

3 What do you like the most about traditional zoos? Modern zoos? What do you like the least? Why?

_____

_____

_____

_____

_____

4 Read the title of the article. What aspect of zoos do you think the reading will focus on?

_____

CD 2
Track 09

Wilder Places for Wild Things

by Sharon Begley with Karen Springen, Jeanne Gordon, Daniel Glick, and Howard Manley, _Newsweek_

1   The beavers at the Minnesota Zoo seem engaged in an unending task. Each week they fell scores of inch-thick young trees for their winter food supply. Each week zoo workers surreptitiously replace the downed trees, anchoring new ones in the iron holders so the animals can keep on cutting. Letting the beavers
5   do what comes naturally has paid off: Minnesota is one of the few zoos to get them to reproduce in captivity. The chimps at the St. Louis Zoo also work for a living: they poke stiff pieces of hay into an anthill to scoop out the baby food and honey that curators hide inside. Instead of idly awaiting banana handouts,

the chimps get to manipulate tools, just as they do in the wild. Last year, when 13 gorillas moved into Zoo Atlanta's new $4.5 million rain forest, they mated and formed families—a rarity among captives. "Zoos have changed from being mere menageries to being celebrations of life," says John Gwynne of the Bronx Zoo. "As the wild places get smaller, the role of zoos gets larger, which means intensifying the naturalness of the experience for both visitors and animals."

Naturalistic zoos are hardly new: animals liberated from concrete cages have been romping on Bronx savannas since 1941. But as species become extinct at a rate unparalleled since the Cretaceous era and 100 acres of tropical forests vanish every minute, zoos are striving to make their settings match their new role as keepers of the biological flame. Since 1980 the nation's 143 accredited zoos and aquariums have spent more than $1 billion on renovation and construction, much of it going to create habitats that immerse both animals and visitors in the sights, sounds, feel and smell of the wild. Today's best exhibits reproduce not just the look but also the function of a natural habitat: they encourage the residents to mate, to raise young and to develop the survival skills they would need on the savannas of Africa or the slopes of the Andes. . . .

Lately, curators have been making exhibits not only look real but sound real. At the Bronx Zoo's lush Jungle World the shrieks of gibbons, the cacophony of crickets and the trills of hornbills emanate from 65 speakers. The zoo's resident audio expert, Tom Veltre, spent a month in Thailand stringing microphones and a mile of cables up and down mountains to capture the sounds of the jungle. Even though the animals figure out that the hoots and howls are coming from black boxes, and not from furry or feathered neighbors, the call of the wild can shape their behavior. At Healesville Sanctuary, outside Melbourne, Australia, nighttime sounds cue nocturnal platypuses when to sleep, says bio-acoustician Leslie Gilbert; realistic noises also snap gorillas out of stress-induced lethargy.

"Natural" is now going beyond sight and sound to include everything from weather to activity patterns. Every day 11 rainstorms hit Tropic World at the Brookfield Zoo outside Chicago, prompting the monkeys to drop from their vines and scamper for cover amid cliffs, 50-foot-high gunite trees and 6,000 tropical plants. Regardless of the climate, the monkeys exhibit an array of behaviors never displayed in cages, such as rustling bushes to define their territories. At the San Diego Zoo's Sun Bear Forest, lion-tailed macaques are surrounded by jungle vines and cascading waterfalls. As soon as these highly endangered monkeys moved in last month, they fanned out and began foraging for fruit and other dainties left by the curators. They even respond to the dominant male's alarm call by clustering around him—something keepers had never seen. At Seattle's Woodland Park Zoo, elephants in the exhibit that opened last month roll and stack logs just as they do in a Thai logging camp. The task relieves the pachyderms' boredom.

50 Curators of rare species are focusing on how to induce one particular natural behavior—reproduction. At New York's Central Park Zoo, which reopened last year after a multimillion-dollar overhaul, the lights in the penguin house mimic seasonal changes in the austral day and night, which serve as a crucial cue for the birds' breeding cycle. At the San Diego Wild Animal Park, people are confined to 55 cages (an electric monorail), and 2,600 animals roam free on 700 acres of veld and savanna. A white rhino that had never mated during 10 years at the San Diego Zoo has sired 55 offspring since moving into a 110-acre area at the park 17 years ago. "The difference is that he has room to mark out his territory and a harem [of 20] from which to choose," says spokesman Tom Hanscom. Getting flamingos 60 to breed was simply a matter of providing more neighbors. For reasons curators can't explain, the leggy pink birds never bred when they lived in two flocks of 50. But when merged into a group of 100 they began to build little mud mounds in the lake shallows on which to lay their eggs.

Once fiercely competitive, most American zoos now participate in species-65 survival programs, intricate dating games for animals living far apart. Coordinated by the American Association of Zoological Parks and Aquariums, the SSP's rely on studbooks that keep track of zoo animals' age and ancestry, helping curators determine how to pair up males and females from member zoos to maintain the species' health and avoid inbreeding. Animals move back 70 and forth between zoos to ensure the best genetic mix. Right now Indian rhinos from the Oklahoma City and National zoos are cozying up to the Bronx Zoo's female.

Without such programs, many species would be extinct. "Zoos are becoming the last hope for a number of endangered species," says Ronald Tilson of the 75 Minnesota Zoo. Indeed, there are more Siberian tigers in America's zoos than on Russia's northern tundra. For all their breeding successes, though, zoos will become little more than Noah's arks if nature continues to give way to pavement. That's why the new naturalistic settings are designed with people in mind, too. "Part of a zoo's reason for being is to inform the public of the 80 marvelous things that occur on this planet," says Warren Thomas, director of the Los Angeles Zoo. "You do that by re-creating the environment that shaped these animals." In zoo parlance, it's called habitat immersion: getting visitors curious and excited about wild places and teaching them that habitat loss is the single greatest threat to wild animals today.

85   In the rare cases when animals bred in captivity do have an ancestral home to return to, zoos are trying to oblige them. "The closer you come to mimicking nature in captivity, the easier that is," says primate curator Ann Baker of Brookfield. Already the Bronx Zoo has returned condors to the Andes. Scientists at the National Zoo in Washington taught a group of golden lion tamarins

90 survival skills, such as how to forage and to heed warning calls, and have released 67 into a reserve near Rio de Janeiro since 1984. Although 35 died, others not only survived but mated; so far, the freed animals have produced 13 surviving offspring. The San Diego Park has returned 49 oryxes—rare antelopes—to Oman, Jordan and Israel, where the graceful creatures have bred

95 successfully. Black-foot ferrets, which a few years ago had dwindled to only 17 in the wild, have proliferated to 125 in captivity, and scientists plan to release the animals into prairie-dog territories in the Great Plains in a few years.

    With every animal that moves onto the endangered species list, or drops off it by extinction, zoos assume greater importance. About 120 million people

100 will visit U.S. zoos this year, giving curators 120 million chances to spread the conservation gospel. By showing how animals are shaped and supported by their environment, "zoos are trying to protect wild places as well as wild things," says Zoo Atlanta director Terry Maple. For as the wild places go, so go the wild animals.

Reading Overview: Main Idea, Details, and Summary

Read the passage again. As you read, underline what you think are the most important ideas. Then, in one or two sentences, write the main idea of the reading. **Use your own words.**

Main Idea

_____

_____

_____

Details

Use the outline below to organize the information in the reading. Refer back to the information you underlined in the passage as a guide. When you have finished, write a brief summary of the reading. **Use your own words.**

I. Examples of Animal Behavior in Naturalistic Settings

    A. _____

    B. _____

    C. _____

II. Zoos Recreate Animals' Natural Environment

    What zoos do: _____

    Examples: _____

    _____

    Results: _____

III. _____

    A. Purpose of the SSPs

        1. _____

        2. _____

        3. _____

B. _____

   1. _____

   2. _the release of golden lion tamarins into a reserve in Brazil_

   3. _____

Summary

_____

_____

_____

_____

_____

B Statement Evaluation

Read the statements. Then scan the article to find out if each sentence is **True (T)**, **False (F)**, or an **Opinion (O)**. Write **T, F,** or **O.**

1 _____ Beavers reproduce in most zoos.

2 _____ At the Minnesota Zoo, animals are able to get their own food instead of being fed.

3 _____ Naturalistic zoos are better than traditional zoos.

4 _____ Modern zoos do not encourage animals to learn how to survive in the wild.

5 _____ Zoo curators are arranging for animals from different zoos to reproduce together.

6 _____ Naturalistic zoos give people important information about an animal's natural environment.

7 _____ Animals are happier in naturalistic zoos than they are in traditional zoos.

Reading Analysis

Read each question carefully. Circle the letter or number of the correct answer, or write the answer.

1 Read lines 6–8.

    a. What do the chimps at this zoo **work for?**

    _____

    b. What follows the **colon (:)?**

        1. An explanation
        2. An example
        3. A new idea

2 Read lines 9–11. What is **a rarity among captives?**

_____

3 Read lines 13–14. **The role of zoos gets larger** means

    a. zoos are getting bigger
    b. zoos are becoming more important
    c. wild places are getting smaller

4 Read lines 26–28. Where do the realistic sounds in the zoos come from?

    a. The jungle
    b. The animals
    c. The speakers

5 Read lines 36–45.

    a. Why is the word **natural** in quotation marks (" ")?

    _____

    b. What does **regardless of** mean?

        1. In spite of
        2. Instead of
        3. In addition to

    c. What does **these highly endangered monkeys** refer to?

    _____

6 Read lines 47–49.

    a. What word is a synonym for **pachyderms?**

    _____

    b. What does **just as** mean?
       1. Only
       2. In the same way
       3. Because of

7 Read lines 64–69. What is an **SSP?**

_____

8 Read lines 85–86. **Zoos are trying to oblige them** means that zoos
    a. want to return animals to their natural environment
    b. want to keep the animals in captivity
    c. are trying to get the animals to reproduce

9 Read lines 95–97. What are **dwindled** and **proliferated?**
    a. Numbers
    b. Synonyms
    c. Antonyms

10 Read lines 98–99.

    a. Animals that **drop off it by extinction**
       1. all die
       2. survive
       3. increase

    b. Read lines 103–104. **For as the wild places go, so go the wild animals,** means that when the animals' natural environment disappears
       1. the animals will reproduce
       2. the animals will disappear, too
       3. the animals will prefer to live in zoos

Dictionary Skills

Read the excerpts from the article. Then read the dictionary entry for the boldfaced word and write the number of the definition that is appropriate for the context. Be prepared to explain your choice.

1 Seasonal changes in the austral day and night serve as a crucial **cue** for the penguins' breeding cycle.

cue: _____

> **cue** **1** **a** : a signal (as a word, phrase, or bit of stage business) to a performer to begin a specific speech or action **b** : something serving a comparable purpose : HINT **2** : a feature indicating the nature of something perceived **3** *archaic* : the part one has to perform in or as if in a play . . .

2 Since 1980 the nation's 143 accredited zoos and aquariums have spent more than $1 billion on renovation and construction, much of it going to create habitats that **immerse** both animals and visitors in the sights, sounds, feel and smell of the wild.

Part of a zoo's reason for being is to inform the public. You do that by re-creating the environment that shaped these animals. This is called habitat **immersion:** getting visitors curious and excited about wild places.

immerse: _____

> **immerse** **1** : to plunge into something that surrounds or covers; *especially* : to plunge or dip into a fluid **2** : ENGROSS, ABSORB <completely *immersed* in his work> **3** : to baptize by immersion

3 The lights in the penguin house **mimic** seasonal changes in the austral day and night.

The closer you can **mimic** nature in captivity, the easier it is to return animals to the wild.

mimic: _____

> **mimic** **1** : to imitate closely : APE **2** : to ridicule by imitation **3** : SIMULATE **4** : to resemble by biological mimicry

4 When animals bred in captivity have a home to return to, zoos are trying to **oblige** them. Already the Bronx Zoo has returned condors to the Andes.

oblige: _____

> **oblige** *transitive verb* **1** : to constrain by physical, moral, or legal force or by the exigencies of circumstance <*obliged* to find a job> **2 a** : to put in one's debt by a favor or service <we are much *obliged* for your help> **b** : to do a favor for <always ready to oblige a friend>
> *intransitive verb* : to do something as or as if as a favor

Word Partnership	Use *obligation* with:
adj.	**legal** obligation, **moral** obligation
n.	**sense of** obligation
v.	obligation **to pay, feel an** obligation, **fulfill an** obligation, **meet an** obligation

E

Critical Thinking Strategies

Read each question carefully, and write a response. Remember that there is no one correct answer. Your response depends on what **you** think.

1 Why have zoos taken on the responsibility of preserving endangered species?

_____

_____

_____

_____

_____

2 The authors state that most American zoos were **once fiercely competitive.** Why were zoos competitive? Why are they not competitive anymore?

_____

_____

_____

_____

_____

3 Why are there more Siberian tigers in America's zoos than there are in Russia's northern tundra?

_____

_____

_____

4 Why do zoos assume greater importance as more animals move onto the endangered species list?

_____

_____

_____

Another Perspective

Read the article and answer the questions that follow.

CD 2
Track 10

Predators on the Prowl

by Marc Peyser with Daniel Glick, *Newsweek*

1   For Iris Kenna, Cuyamaga Rancho State Park near San Diego was like a second home. By day she strolled its fields in search of exotic birds. At night, the 56-year-old high-school counselor sometimes slept under the stars. But one morning exactly a year ago, Kenna encountered something unfamiliar, and it

5   saw her first. Without warning, a 140-pound male mountain lion pounced on her from behind. The struggle was brief. The animal dragged the dying 5-foot-4 Kenna into dense brush to hide her from competing predators. Rangers found her only after two hikers spotted a pair of glasses, a backpack and a human tooth by the path she had been on. The rangers followed a trail of her clothes for

10   30 yards until they came to Kenna's body. The back of her scalp was ripped off; the rest of her was riddled with bites. No one had heard a scream, or even a roar.

Kenna is the most vivid symbol of an angry, shifting debate over how people and predators can coexist. In the high-growth Western states, many residents love living near the wild, and they are inclined to preserve it no matter what

15   the risks. But violent deaths like Kenna's—and a string of other mountain lion attacks—are making a powerful case for fighting back. Californians will vote in March on opening the way to mountain lion hunting, which has been prohibited there for more than 20 years.[1] But Oregon, Arizona and Colorado recently changed their hunting laws to ensure that predatory animals—including bears, wolves and coyotes—would be protected. "It's overwhelmingly popular to have

20   these animals in our ecosystems," says Tom Dougherty of the National Wildlife Federation. "But if they're in your backyard, some people aren't loving it."

The most acute mountain lion problem is in California. That's partly because the state's human population has doubled every 25 years this century. As more people built more houses, they usurped territory once largely inhabited by wild

25   animals. But the mountain lion (alternately called cougar, puma and panther) has also been questionably served by environmentalists. In 1972, preservation-minded Californians banned hunting the majestic animals (except when they pose an imminent danger to people or livestock). The cougar population

[1] Postscript: In March, Californians once again voted against legalization of mountain lion hunting.

30 ballooned, from an estimated 2,400 lions to 6,000 today. Without hunters to thin the ranks, increased competition for food has sent hungry mountain lions to suburban backyards, shopping centers and elementary schools in search of nourishment—a deer or, lacking that, a dog. Even children have been mauled. "People are afraid to go on a picnic without taking a firearm," says state Senator
35 Timi Leslie, a prominent anti-cougar advocate. In the wake of Kenna's death, Governor Pete Wilson authorized the March ballot initiative—one that could lead to controlling the cougar population.

But in other places, sentiment favors animals at least as much as people. A survey of Coloradans living near the Rockies found that 80 percent believe
40 that development in mountain lion territory should be restricted. What's more, when wildlife authorities killed the cougar that killed a woman named Barbara Schoener in California, donors raised $21,000 to care for the cougar's cub—but only $9,000 for Schoener's two children.

1 How did Iris Kenna die?

_____

2 **a.** What proposed law must Californians decide upon?

_____

b. What is the purpose of this proposed law?

_____

_____

c. Why are some people against this proposed law?

_____

_____

3 Why has the mountain lion problem in California increased over the years?

_____

_____

_____

UNIT 4   THE ENVIRONMENT

4 How do most people in Colorado feel about the mountain lions? What example do the authors give to support this?

_____

_____

5 What is the authors' opinion of the mountain lion situation in the western United States? Explain your answer.

_____

_____

_____

G Topics for Discussions and Writing

1 According to the article, "Wilder Places for Wild Things," a number of endangered species raised in zoos were released into the wild, but many of these animals died. Do you think it is worth the risk for zoos to release these endangered animals into the wild? Discuss your opinion with your classmates.

2 Compare the zoos in this country with zoos in your country and in other countries. How are they similar? How are they different?

3 Many zoo curators and other specialists are trying to save species of animals from extinction. Do you think it is important to try to preserve these animals? Explain your point of view.

4 **Write in your journal.** Refer to "Predators on the Prowl." Think about the amount of money that was raised for Barbara Schoener's two children compared to the money raised to care for the cougar's cub. What is your opinion about this?

Follow-up Activities

1. Refer to the **Self-Evaluation of Reading Strategies** on page 240. Check off the strategies you used to understand "Wilder Places for Wild Things." Think about the strategies you didn't use, and apply them to help you understand the readings that follow.

2. Work in small groups. You are journalists for a local television station in San Diego. You have been assigned to cover the use of state and municipal (i.e. local) funds that have recently been allocated to the San Diego Zoo. Prepare an interview with the curator of the San Diego Zoo. In your interview, include questions about the justification of this money for the zoo's long-range goals. For example, what will the zoo do with the money? Why should the zoo have gotten such funding? Why should the residents of San Diego and California support such a project? Remember to add some questions of your own. When you have finished, exchange your questions with another group. Try to answer each other's questions. When you are finished, compare your responses. Have the "curators" answered the "interviewers'" questions convincingly?

3. Work in small groups. What do you think of the problem described in "Predators on the Prowl"? How can the problem be solved? Write a list of your group's suggestions. Then compare your list with your classmates'. Decide which two or three solutions are the best.

Cloze Quiz

Complete the passage with words from the list. Use each word only once.

beavers	extinct	natural	sounds
behaviors	habitats	replace	vanish
construction	hide	reproduce	visitors
cue	mated	role	weather
elephants	mimic	smaller	work

The beavers at the Minnesota Zoo seem engaged in an unending task. Each week they fell scores of inch-thick young trees for their winter food supply. Each week zoo workers _____ the downed trees, anchoring
(1)
new ones in the iron holders so the animals can keep on cutting. Letting the _____ do what comes naturally has paid off: Minnesota is one
(2)
of the few zoos to get them to _____ in captivity. The chimps at
(3)
the St. Louis Zoo also _____ for a living: they poke stiff pieces
(4)
of hay into an anthill to scoop out the baby food and honey that curators _____ inside. Instead of idly awaiting banana handouts, the
(5)
chimps get to manipulate tools, just as they do in the wild. Last year, when 13 gorillas moved into Zoo Atlanta's new $4.5 million rain forest, they _____ and formed families—a rarity among captives. "Zoos
(6)
have changed from being mere menageries to being celebrations of life," says John Gwynne of the Bronx Zoo. "As the wild places get _____
(7)
the role of zoos gets larger, which means intensifying the naturalness of the experience for both _____ and animals."
(8)

Naturalistic zoos are hardly new; animals liberated from concrete cages have been romping on Bronx savannas since 1941. But as species become _____ at a rate unparalleled since the Cretaceous era and
(9)
100 acres of tropical forests _____ every minute, zoos are
(10)
striving to make their settings match their new _____ as
(11)
keepers of the biological flame. Since 1980 the nation's 143 accredited zoos and aquariums have spent more than $1 billion on renovation and _____ , much of it going to create _____ that
(12)   (13)
immerse both animals and visitors in the sights, _____ , feel
(14)
and smell of the wild. Today's best exhibits reproduce not just the look but also the function of a _____ habitat: they encourage the
(15)
residents to mate, to raise young and to develop the survival skills they would need on the savannas of Africa or the slopes of the Andes. . . .

"Natural" is now going beyond sight and sound to include everything from _____ to activity patterns. Every day 11 rainstorms
(16)
hit Tropic World at the Brookfield Zoo outside Chicago, prompting the monkeys to drop from their vines and scamper for cover amid cliffs, 50-foot-high trees and 6,000 tropical plants. Regardless of the climate, the monkeys exhibit an array of _____ never displayed in cages, such as
(17)
rustling bushes to define their territories. At Seattle's Woodland Park Zoo, _____ in the exhibit that opened last month roll and stack logs
(18)
just as they do in a Thai logging camp. The task relieves the pachyderms' boredom.

Curators of rare species are focusing on how to induce one particular natural behavior—reproduction. At New York's Central Park Zoo, which reopened last year after a multimillion-dollar overhaul, the lights in the penguin house _____ seasonal changes in the austral day and

(19)
night, which serve as a crucial _____ for the birds' breeding

(20)
cycle. At the San Diego Wild Animal Park, people are confined to cages (an electric monorail), and 2,600 animals roam free on 700 acres of veld and savanna. A white rhino that had never mated during 10 years at the San Diego Zoo has sired 55 offspring since moving into a 110-acre area at the park 17 years ago.

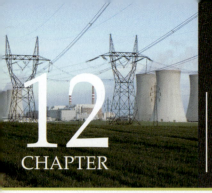

12
CHAPTER

A Nuclear Graveyard

Prereading Preparation

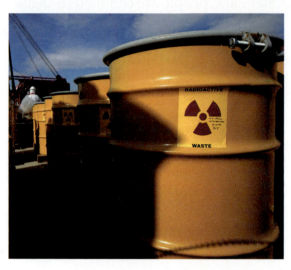

One of the greatest environmental concerns facing the world today is the disposal of nuclear waste. Much of this waste comes from nuclear power plants. (Refer to the illustration on page 240. You may want to do the exercise related to the illustration before you read the article.) In the United States, for example, the government is looking for a safe place to bury its nuclear waste. Currently, the federal government is focusing on one site: the Yucca Mountains in Nevada. Read the following paragraph, which is the first part of the article. Then answer the questions.

CD 2
Track 11

A Nuclear Graveyard

by Betsy Carpenter, *U.S. News & World Report*

1. The apocalyptic scenario begins with an earthquake near Yucca Mountain, a barren ridge 90 miles northwest of Las Vegas that is the burial site for the nation's most lethal nuclear waste. The tremor is minor; but fresh movement in the earth's crust causes ground water to well up suddenly, flooding the

5 repository. Soon, a lethal brew of nuclear poisons seeps into the water that flows underground to nearby Death Valley. Insects, birds and animals drink at the valley's contaminated springs, and slowly the radioactivity spreads into the biosphere. "It would be a terrible disaster," says Charles Archambeau, a geophysicist at the University of Colorado.

1 What does this paragraph describe?

  a. It describes what may happen if there is an earthquake at the place where the nuclear waste is buried.

  b. It describes what happens during all earthquakes.

2 Work with a partner to complete the flowchart. According to the first paragraph of "A Nuclear Graveyard," what is the chain of events that would lead to **radioactivity spreading into the biosphere?**

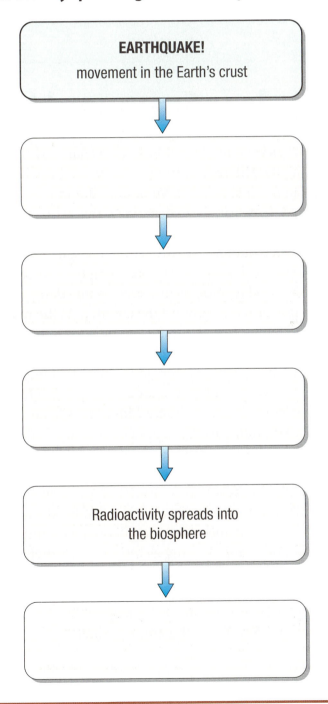

EARTHQUAKE!

movement in the Earth's crust

Radioactivity spreads into the biosphere

3 Do you think there is a better way for a country to dispose of its nuclear waste? Write your ideas on the lines below. Then discuss them with your classmates. Make a list of the class's solutions. Then continue reading the article.

_____

_____

_____

CD 2
Track 12

A Nuclear Graveyard (continued)

10   Much has been made of this scary scenario by the state of Nevada, which is fighting the federal government's plan to bury all the nation's high-level nuclear refuse inside Yucca Mountain. But in fact, the risk to Nevadans may be overstated. Increasingly, experts view this arid, desolate ridge as a good spot for
15   a permanent nuclear graveyard. The threat to Americans posed by the federal government's bungled attempts to find a safe burial site for the waste looms large, however. Thousands of tons of highly radioactive spent fuel rods rest temporarily today in pools of water—some dangerously overcrowded—near nuclear power plants around the country. At the nation's weapons factories,
20   corroding tanks are leaking nuclear poisons into the ground water. This stalemate over nuclear waste is strangling the nuclear power industry, and experts are increasingly troubled by the possibility that nuclear waste could become the weapon of choice for a new breed of terrorist.
      The twin virtues of the Yucca Mountain site are its remoteness and aridity.
25   From the summit, the only sign of civilization is the dusty trace of a dirt road cutting across a brown, barren valley. The ridge is located on the southwest corner of the Nevada Test Site, where the government explodes nuclear weapons, so access is tightly restricted. Sagebrush, creosote bushes and other desert plants attest to the locale's remarkable dryness.
30   Indeed, only six inches of rain fall on the mountain each year, and most of the moisture evaporates, leaving as little as one fiftieth of an inch to soak into the ground. The water table is unusually deep, more than one third of a mile below the surface. According to the Department of Energy, which is charged with building the repository, nuclear waste could be buried far beneath the ground
35   yet still rest safely above the ground water.

Geological Turmoil

The landscape also provides stark reminders of why critics are so concerned. To the southeast stands Busted Butte, a peak that was sheared in half long ago by earthquakes; to the west, four smooth-sloped volcanoes rise out of a high valley. The reason for the geological turmoil is that immense forces inside the earth are stretching the earth's crust apart here, much like a sheet of rubber. Earthquakes relieve the strain, but they also disrupt the water table: As the crust snaps back into shape, rocks contract, and water that has seeped deep into fractures is forced up toward the surface.

The repository site must be capable of isolating atomic waste for 10,000 years. By all accounts, there could be a frightful mess if the poisons escaped the site. In just a few years, the nation has already produced 48,000 tons of high-level nuclear waste, the most concentrated products of the nuclear era. Every speck of this refuse is intensely poisonous.

Water is the worst enemy of buried nuclear waste. If water did find its way into the repository, it would corrode the storage canisters and hasten the escape of radioactive particles through the rock. Scientists cannot know absolutely whether ground water will well up under Yucca Mountain during the next 10,000 years. The calculation simply has too many unknowns: A new ice age, global climate change, erosion, volcanoes and earthquakes all could affect the water table. To gauge the probabilities, scientists reconstruct the past. If the water table has risen in the past, scientists assume, it is likely to do so again.

Jerry Szymanski, a maverick engineering geologist with the Department of Energy (DOE), claims that he has rock-hard evidence that ground water was once as much as 500 meters higher than it is today. He has devoted the past seven years to blowing the whistle on what he believes to be a fatally flawed site, and his arguments have received extensive media attention. Szymanski bases his case largely on the presence of thick, cream-colored veins of a crystalline deposit, known as calcite, that plunge through the mottled, grey bedrock of Yucca Mountain. In Szymanski's view, these calcite brands must have been deposited slowly, layer by layer, as mineral-rich ground water welled up into fractures in the rock. "Ground water will rise again in the next 10,000 years," he says flatly. "It is as certain as death."

Other Voices

But according to an increasing number of earth scientists, it is not the site but Szymanski's conclusion that is fatally flawed. Largely as a result of Szymanski's warnings, the National Academy of Sciences convened a panel of researchers to evaluate the risks associated with ground water. The panel has not yet released its final report, but already many members are convinced that there is no evidence for Szymanski's hypothesis—but there are several good reasons to doubt it. Most believe that rainwater, not upwelling ground water, probably produced the calcite veins. One strong reason to suspect precipitation, says Bob Fournier, a geologist with the United States Geological Survey in Menlo Park, California, is that the calcite veins around Yucca Mountain do not exhibit the common structural characteristics of ancient springs. For instance, upwelling water typically leaves snowy-white mounds of calcite on the ground, deposits that are formed when the water evaporates; few such signatures can be found at Yucca Mountain.

Preliminary chemical analyses also suggest that the disputed calcites were deposited by rainwater. Doug Rumble, a geochemist at the Carnegie Institution in Washington, D.C., analyzed several existing studies of the chemical character of the disputed Yucca Mountain veins, the ground water underneath and ancient and modern ground water deposits; he found no evidence that the calcites at Yucca are or ever were caused by ground water.

Somewhat surprisingly, scientists are much more concerned about ground water seepage than they are about more dramatic geologic events like volcanoes and earthquakes. Fresh eruptions from the small volcanoes along Yucca Mountain's western flank probably wouldn't threaten the repository because the flows would be small and localized, most geologists believe. The possibility of a direct hit, a new upwelling of magma right beneath the repository, is minute, they say.

Earthquakes are not a major concern either, scientists contend. Though Yucca Mountain is ringed with seismic faults, many of them known to be active, most geologists do not worry that shock waves from an earthquake could rupture the repository. Experience with tremors throughout the world has shown unequivocally that tunnels and mines stand up well to them. For instance, a devastating earthquake killed 250,000 people in a coal-mining city in China in 1976. Reportedly, workers in the mines below did not feel even the slightest tremor. Closer to home, underground nuclear explosions on the nearby test site have shown that tunnels can withstand forces even greater than those produced by earthquakes.

"From what we know now, I would feel quite comfortable with Yucca Mountain," says George Thompson, a geologist at Stanford University and a member of the National Academy of Sciences' panel. Though panel members agree that a lot more study is needed, most do not believe that the geological complexity disqualifies the site. Explains Clarence Allen, a geologist from Caltech in Pasadena, California, "If you asked me to find a site with fewer earthquakes or volcanoes, I could. But an overall better site? I'm not so sure."

Maintaining the pretense of an unassailable site also has had an unfortunate impact on the design of the repository. Currently, the DOE plans to build a complex that would be backfilled and sealed off after it had been loaded to capacity. Experts like Stanford's George Thompson assert that this approach is foolish. Instead, the government should design the facility so that the waste could be easily retrieved if the repository failed.

Congress must have had an inkling that forcing the project on Nevada might not work out in the end. In the same bill that designated Yucca Mountain the sole candidate for site evaluation, Congress established the Office of the U.S. Nuclear Waste Negotiator, which is charged with finding a willing state or Indian tribe[1] to host the repository. David Leroy, who took the job last summer, is putting together a package of incentives and assurances that he hopes will lure several state or tribal leaders to the bargaining table. The assurances include promises of local participation in deciding how the facility is operated and the freedom to back out of the evaluation process at any time. When it comes to incentives the sky's the limit. Highways? Airports? Schools? Harbor cleanups? "You tell me what the problem is, and let's see if we can address it," he says. Who knows, maybe Leroy can find a way to make even cynical Nevadans willing to host the repository.

[1] In the United States, Indian (Native American) tribes own their land, called *reservations*. The tribe holds decision-making power as to what takes place on tribal land. They are not under the jurisdiction of the federal government or of the government of the state in which the reservation is located.

Reading Overview: Main Idea, Details, and Summary

Read the passage again. As you read, underline what you think are the most important ideas. Then, in one or two sentences, write the main idea of the reading. **Use your own words.**

Main Idea

_____

_____

_____

Details

Use the chart below to organize the information in the article. Refer back to the information you underlined in the passage as a guide. When you have finished, write a brief summary of the reading. **Use your own words.**

The Nuclear Repository Controversy: To Use or Not to Use the Yucca Mountain Site	
Arguments Against Using the Yucca Mountain Site	Arguments in Favor of Using the Yucca Mountain Site

Summary

_____

_____

_____

_____

_____

B

Statement Evaluation

Read the statements. Then scan the article to find out if each sentence is **True (T), False (F),** or an **Inference (I).** Write **T, F,** or **I.**

1 _____ Experts believe that Yucca Mountain is a good place to bury nuclear waste.

2 _____ There is a great deal of rain on the mountain every year.

3 _____ The greatest danger to nuclear waste is water.

4 _____ The presence of calcite has led to many arguments about the safety of Yucca Mountain as a nuclear waste repository site.

5 _____ Earthquake tremors are always felt far below the surface of the earth.

6 _____ Most members of the National Academy of Sciences' panel believe that the Yucca Mountain site may be a good place for nuclear waste disposal.

7 _____ Some Indian tribes live near Yucca Mountain.

Reading Analysis

Read each question carefully. Circle the letter or number of the correct answer, or write the answer.

1 In line 10, what does **this scary scenario** refer to?

_____

2 Read lines 12–13.

a. **The risk to Nevadans may be overstated.** To **overstate** means

1. to make something seem greater than it really is
2. to make something seem smaller than it really is

b. Who are **Nevadans?**

_____

3 Read lines 24–29.

a. **Remoteness** means

1. close to people
2. far away from people

b. How do you know?

_____

c. In this paragraph, what is a synonym of **aridity?**

_____

4 Read lines 33–35. What is a **repository?**

a. Nuclear waste
b. A safe place for the nuclear waste
c. The ground water above the nuclear waste

5 Read lines 44–48. Which word is a synonym of **waste?**

_____

6 Read lines 49–56.

a. Why do scientists reconstruct the past?

1. To predict what may happen in the future
2. To help them understand the past

    b. **It is likely to do so again** means

      1. there may be more earthquakes
      2. the water table may rise again
      3. the climate may change again

7 Read lines 59–61. **Blowing the whistle** means

    a. making music
    b. giving false information
    c. revealing the truth

8 Read lines 74–78. What is one type of **precipitation** referred to in these lines?

_____

9 Read lines 92–94.

    a. A **direct hit** refers to

      1. an earthquake
      2. a volcano erupting
      3. water seepage

    b. **The possibility of a direct hit … is minute** means

      1. there is a very small chance of a direct hit
      2. there is a very big chance of a direct hit

10 Read lines 95–104.

    a. **Unequivocally** means

      1. probably
      2. definitely
      3. slightly

    b. What is an example of the **unequivocal** evidence that tunnels and mines are not damaged by earthquakes?

_____

_____

11 Read lines 118–122.

    a. What is the job of the Office of the U.S. Nuclear Waste Negotiator?

_____

_____

b. In this sentence, **charged with** means

   1. to be made to pay for something
   2. to be suspected of a crime
   3. to be given responsibility for something

12 Read lines 122–127.

a. What are some of the **incentives** David Leroy may offer?

_____

_____

b. What are some of the **assurances** David Leroy may offer?

_____

_____

c. An **incentive** is a

   1. guarantee
   2. motivation
   3. freedom

d. An **assurance** is a

   1. guarantee
   2. motivation
   3. freedom

e. **To lure** means to

   1. attract
   2. buy
   3. discourage

f. **The sky is the limit** means

   1. he won't agree to build airplanes
   2. he will agree to construct tall buildings
   3. anything is possible

Dictionary Skills

Read the excerpts from the article. Then read the dictionary entry for the boldfaced word and write the number of the definition that is appropriate for the context. Be prepared to explain your choice.

PART 1

1. By all **accounts,** there could be a frightful mess if the poisons escaped the site.

   account: _____

   > **account** **1** *archaic* : RECKONING, COMPUTATION **2** **a** : a record of debit and credit entries to cover transactions involving a particular item or a particular person or concern **b** : a statement of transactions during a fiscal period and the resulting balance **3** **a** : a statement explaining one's conduct **b** : a statement or exposition of reasons, causes, or motives <no satisfactory account of these phenomena> **c** : a reason for an action : BASIS <on that account I must refuse> **4** **a** : a formal business arrangement providing for regular dealings or services (as banking, advertising, or store credit) and involving the establishment and maintenance of an account; *also* : CLIENT, CUSTOMER **b** : money deposited in a bank account and subject to withdrawal by the depositor . . . **7** **a** : careful thought : CONSIDERATION <have to take many things into account> **b** : a usually mental record : TRACK <keep account of all you do> **8** : a description of facts, conditions, or events : REPORT, NARRATIVE <the newspaper account of the fire> <by all accounts they're well-off>; *also* : PERFORMANCE <a straightforward account of the sonata> . . .

2. Experts view Yucca Mountain, which is an arid, **desolate** ridge, as a good spot for a permanent nuclear graveyard.

   desolate: _____

   > **desolate** **1** : devoid of inhabitants and visitors : DESERTED **2** : joyless, disconsolate, and sorrowful through or as if through separation from a loved one <a desolate widow> **3** **a** : showing the effects of abandonment and neglect : DILAPIDATED <a desolate old house> **b** : BARREN, LIFELESS <a desolate landscape> **c** : devoid of warmth, comfort, or hope : GLOOMY <desolate memories>

By permission. From *Merriam-Webster's Collegiate® Dictionary*, 11th Edition © 2010 by Merriam-Webster, Incorporated (www.Merriam-Webster.com).

3 The Office of the U.S. Nuclear Waste Negotiator is charged with finding a willing state or Indian tribe to be a **host** for the repository.

host: _____

> **host** **1** **a** : one that receives or entertains guests socially, commercially, or officially **b** : one that provides facilities for an event or function <our college served as host for the basketball tournament> **2** **a** : a living animal or plant on or in which a parasite lives **b** : the larger, stronger, or dominant member of a commensal or symbiotic pair **c** : an individual into which a tissue, part, or embryo is transplanted from another **3** : a mineral or rock that is older than the minerals or rocks in it; *also* : a substance that contains a usually small amount of another substance incorporated in its structure **4** : a radio or television emcee . . .

4 Thousands of tons of highly radioactive **spent** fuel rods rest temporarily today in pools of water near nuclear power plants around the country.

spent: _____

> **spent** **1** **a** : used up : CONSUMED **b** : exhausted of active or required components or qualities often for a particular purpose <spent nuclear fuel> **2** : drained of energy or effectiveness : EXHAUSTED **3** : exhausted of spawn or sperm <spent fishes>

PART 2

Sometimes a word not only has different meanings; it also has different pronunciations depending on the meaning. For example, in this chapter, the words **minute** and **refuse** each have several meanings and two different pronunciations. Read the entries for these words carefully and choose the most appropriate definition for the context. Check with your teacher to make sure that you pronounce the words correctly, depending on the meaning.

5 The possibility of a direct hit by an earthquake, and a new upwelling of magma right beneath the repository, is **minute,** according to scientists.

minute: _____

> **minute** **1** : very small : INFINITESIMAL **2** : of small importance : TRIFLING **3** : marked by close attention to details

By permission. From *Merriam-Webster's Collegiate® Dictionary*, 11th Edition © 2010 by Merriam-Webster, Incorporated (www.Merriam-Webster.com).

UNIT 4   THE ENVIRONMENT

6 The U.S. government plans to bury the nation's high-level nuclear **refuse** inside Yucca Mountain in Nevada.

In just a few years, the nation has already produced 48,000 tons of high-level nuclear waste. Every speck of this **refuse** is intensely poisonous.

refuse: _____

refuse **1** : the worthless or useless part of something : LEAVINGS **2** : TRASH, GARBAGE

Word Partnership	Use *account* with:
n.	**bank** account, account **number,** account **balance, savings** account
v.	**access your** account, **open an** account, **give a detailed** account, **take** *something* **into** account
adj.	**blow-by-blow** account

E

Critical Thinking Strategies

Read each question carefully, and write a response. Remember that there is no one correct answer. Your response depends on what **you** think.

1 Does Betsy Carpenter, the author of this article, believe that there are sufficient reasons for not using Yucca Mountain as a nuclear waste site? Explain your answer.

_____

_____

_____

_____

_____

2   Jerry Szymanski, who is a geologist, and "a number of earth scientists, also geologists," disagree on the interpretation of the same evidence, i.e., the calcite veins in the bedrock of Yucca Mountain. Why might Nevadans be unhappy with these conflicting interpretations of the same data?

_____

_____

_____

_____

_____

3   According to the article, **The repository site must be capable of isolating atomic waste for 10,000 years,** the length of time the waste material remains radioactive. What implications might you draw from this concern that the site remain intact for the full 10,000 years that it remains contaminated?

_____

_____

_____

_____

_____

4   Does the government believe that most people would be willing to have a nuclear repository in their state? Explain your answer.

_____

_____

_____

_____

_____

Another Perspective

Map of the United States Indicating Distances from Yucca Mountain

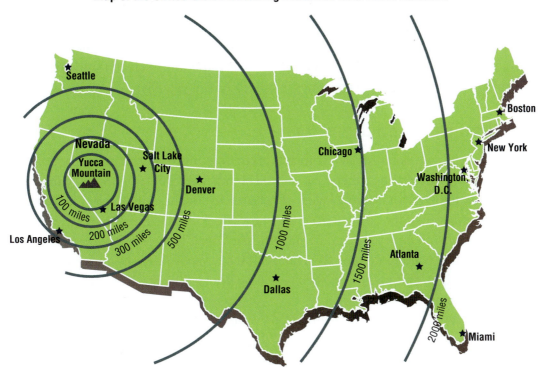

Read the article and answer the questions that follow.

CD 2
Track 13

A Nuclear Graveyard (excerpt)

1   The biggest problem at Yucca Mountain may be local opposition fomented in part by federal mishandling of the site-selection process. Nine years ago, Congress passed the Nuclear Waste Policy Act. In 1983, the DOE selected nine sites around the country for consideration as a possible repository. A couple of years later, the

5   list was narrowed down to three—Yucca Mountain, Hanford, Washington, and Deaf Smith County, Texas. Then, in 1987, Congress ordered the DOE to focus solely on Yucca Mountain, a move that Nevadans feel was made for political reasons: Nevada

has one of the smallest delegations on Capitol Hill.[1] Today, anti-dump sentiment runs deep. Fully four out of five Nevadans oppose the project.

Nevadans are also unnerved by the DOE's horrible environmental record and long-standing culture of secrecy. Indeed, billions of gallons of radioactive and toxic materials were dumped secretly over the past few decades at weapons factories around the country. According to a recent report by the Congressional Office of Technology Assessment, the DOE's two-year-old effort to clean up the mess left on and under DOE weapons facilities is proceeding abysmally.

Changing Benchmarks

In their own defense, DOE officials argue that it is unfair to judge past practices by today's more stringent environmental standards. Moreover, they say the Yucca Mountain project has many layers of external oversight, unlike the weapons facilities that were cloaked in secrecy from the start. The DOE has a point. Every aspect of site evaluation will be scrutinized by the Nuclear Waste Technical Review Board, a panel of experts recommended by the National Academy of Sciences and appointed by the President. Ultimately, the facility will be licensed by the U.S. Nuclear Regulatory Commission.

But Nevadans have a case when they argue that their state has much to lose and little to gain by hosting the site. With its booming economy, Las Vegas doesn't need the 3,000 jobs the facility would provide during construction. Also, a nuclear accident, even a minor one, could harm the Silver State's gaming-based economy by keeping tourists away.

Many critics believe that the very notion of a site that could be "safe" for 10,000 years is ridiculous, and this has intensified local opposition. Science simply cannot prove that a site will be safe for such a long period of time, and citizens know it and feel as if they are being conned, says Frank Parker, chairman of the National Academy of Sciences' Board of Radioactive Waste Management. Parker holds that a more honest—and in the end more reassuring—assessment that the government could have offered Nevadans is that the likelihood of a catastrophic breach is very slim and that the DOE is prepared to act swiftly if problems occur.

[1] Capitol Hill, in Washington, D.C., is the site of the Capitol building, where Congress, consisting of the Senate and the House of Representatives, meets to make laws. The number of representatives each state has is based on its population so that the least populated states have the fewest representatives and consequently, less voice in the House.

1 According to Nevadans, why was Yucca Mountain chosen as the best site for the repository? What does the author imply when she says that Nevada has one of the smallest delegations on Capitol Hill?

_____

_____

_____

2 Why do many people in Nevada oppose the dumping of nuclear waste in that state? What are their concerns?

_____

_____

_____

3 How has the DOE said it would handle the Yucca Mountain situation differently than it handled other projects (for example, weapons facilities) in the past?

_____

_____

_____

4 What business does the economy of Nevada depend on? How might this business be affected by nuclear dumping?

_____

_____

_____

Topics for Discussion and Writing

G

1 Work in pairs or small groups. Look carefully at the following map. What observations can you make about the number and location of nuclear power plants throughout the world? When you are finished, write a composition describing your conclusions.

Number of Nuclear Reactors in Operation Worldwide
(February 2009)

North America — 124
Europe — 151
Asia — 155
Africa — 2
South America — 4
Australia — 0
Antarctica — 0

2 If the government wanted to bury a nuclear repository in your state or province, how would you feel? Why? Write a letter to the editor of your local newspaper either in favor of or against the government's proposal.

3 In what other ways can governments dispose of nuclear waste? Discuss your ideas with your class. When you are finished, write a composition. Which ideas do you think are best? Explain your viewpoint.

4 **Write in your journal.** Do you think that the disposal of nuclear waste should be the responsibility of an individual country, or do you think it is a global issue? Explain your reasons. You may also want to discuss whether *all* environmental issues, including the destruction of rain forests, are the joint concern of all countries.

Follow-up Activities

1 Refer to the **Self-Evaluation of Reading Strategies** below. Check off the strategies you used to understand "A Nuclear Graveyard." Evaluate your strategy use throughout the book. Which strategies have you begun to use consistently? Which strategies have you added to the list? Which strategies are becoming automatic? To what extent have you applied these strategies to other reading you do?

Self-Evaluation of Reading Strategies			
	Readings		
Strategies	"Sustainable Farming"	"Wilder Places for Wild Things"	"A Nuclear Graveyard"
I read the title and try to predict what the reading will be about.			
I use my knowledge of the world to help me understand the text.			
I read as though I *expect* the text to have meaning.			
I use illustrations to help me understand the text.			
I ask myself questions about the text.			
I use a variety of types of context clues.			
I take chances in order to identify meaning.			
I continue if I am not successful.			
I identify and underline main ideas.			
I connect details with main ideas.			
I summarize the reading in my own words.			
I skip unnecessary words.			
I look up words correctly in the dictionary.			
I connect the reading to other material I have read.			
I do not translate into my native language.			

2 Look carefully at the illustration below. Read the sentences describing how a nuclear reactor operates. Then match the sentences to the appropriate letter in the illustration.

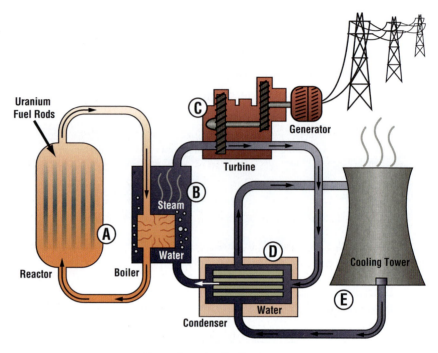

Operation of a Typical Nuclear Power Plant

_____ Hot coolant is piped through the boiler, where it heats water to steam.

_____ Steam drives the turbine, which generates electricity.

_____ In the cooling tower, water is cooled in air, recovered, and pumped through the condenser.

_____ In the reactor core, the radioactive fuel rods generate high temperatures, superheating a liquid coolant.

_____ Steam from the turbine is cooled back to water in the condenser, where it is recycled for use as steam.

3 Work in two groups. The first group represents the Office of the U.S. Nuclear Waste Negotiator. This group will make a list of incentives and assurances to convince the other group to allow the government to build a nuclear repository in their state. The second group represents the citizens of the state where the government wants to bury nuclear waste. This group will make a list of their concerns and demands. When the lists are completed, the students from both groups will discuss how to negotiate and compromise so that both groups are satisfied.

Cloze Quiz

Complete the passage with words from the list. Use each word only once.

assurances	government	nuclear	repository
buried	host	poisonous	road
earthquakes	incentives	radioactive	site
finding	lure	refuse	water
geologist	Nevada	remoteness	years

The state of Nevada is fighting the federal government's plan to bury all the nation's high-level nuclear _____ inside Yucca Mountain.
(1)

But in fact, the risk to Nevadans may be overstated. Increasingly, experts view this arid, desolate ridge as a good spot for a permanent _____
(2)

graveyard. The threat to Americans posed by the federal government's bungled attempts to find a safe burial _____ for the waste
(3)

looms large, however. Thousands of tons of highly _____ spent
(4)

fuel rods rest temporarily today in pools of _____ near nuclear
(5)

power plants around the country.

The twin virtues of the Yucca Mountain site are its _____
(6)

and aridity. From the summit, the only sign of civilization is the dusty trace of a dirt _____ cutting across a brown, barren valley. The
(7)

ridge is located on the southwest corner of the Nevada Test Site, where the

_____ explodes nuclear weapons, so access is tightly restricted.
(8)

The landscape also provides stark reminders of why critics are so concerned. To the southeast stands Busted Butte, a peak that was sheared in half long ago by _____ ; to the west, four smooth-sloped
(9)

volcanoes rise out of a high valley. The reason for the geological turmoil is that immense forces inside the earth are stretching the earth's crust apart here. Earthquakes relieve the strain, but they also disrupt the water table.

The _____ (10) site must be capable of isolating atomic waste for 10,000 _____ (11) . By all accounts, there could be a frightful mess if the poisons escaped the site. In just a few years, the nation has already produced 48,000 tons of high-level nuclear waste, the most concentrated products of the nuclear era. Every speck of this refuse is intensely

_____ (12) .

Water is the worst enemy of _____ (13) nuclear waste. If water did find its way into the repository, it would corrode the storage canisters and hasten the escape of radioactive particles through the rock. Scientists cannot know absolutely whether ground water will well up under Yucca Mountain during the next 10,000 years.

"From what we know now, I would feel quite comfortable with Yucca Mountain," says George Thompson, a _____ (14) at Stanford University and a member of the National Academy of Sciences' panel. Though panel members agree that a lot more study is needed, most do not believe that the geological complexity disqualifies the site.

Congress must have had an inkling in 1987 that forcing the project on _____ (15) might not work out in the end. In the same bill that designated Yucca Mountain the sole candidate for site evaluation, Congress established the Office of the U.S. Nuclear Waste Negotiator, which is charged with _____ (16) a willing state or Indian tribe to _____ (17) the repository. David Leroy, who took the job last summer, is putting together a package of _____ (18) and assurances that he hopes will _____ (19) several state or tribal leaders to the bargaining table. The _____ (20) include promises of local participation in deciding how the facility is operated and the freedom to back out of the evaluation process at any time.

Crossword Puzzle

Read the clues on the next page. Write the answers in the correct spaces in the puzzle.

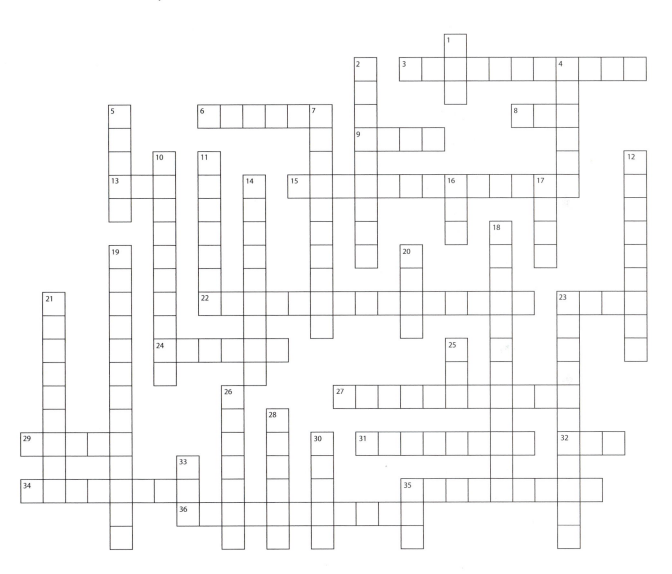

Crossword Puzzle Clues

3. Increase greatly in number

6. Do something as a favor

8. The opposite of **on**

9. Many Nevadans _____ that no waste repository will be built in their state.

13. The past tense of **eat**

15. Capable of naturally breaking down into harmless materials

22. Wind and solar power are _____ friendly. They do not cause air pollution.

23. _____ are animals used to plow fields and pull heavy loads.

24. John's house is in a very _____ location. I would not want to be so distant from other people.

27. Not paying attention

29. Imitate closely

31. A tiger is a _____. It hunts other animals for food.

32. I _____ speak English very well.

34. Deserted; not populated

35. A very surprising or shocking fact

36. Capable of being maintained

1. Girl, _____ , woman, man

2. An elephant

4. Waste

5. A _____ panel uses energy from the sun to generate power.

7. Many wild animals are in danger of _____. They may cease to exist.

10. A storage site is a _____.

11. Diminish; decrease in number

12. A guarantee

14. Animals that are kept in zoos are in _____. They are not free.

16. Each; every

17. Attract

18. What are the practical _____ of this theory?

19. Definitely

20. John and I _____ our vegetable garden with great care.

21. A motivation

23. We only buy _____ grown food, not food grown with chemical fertilizers.

25. Susan waved her hand as a _____ , or signal, for Ann to come into the room.

26. Engross; absorb

28. Mountain lion; puma

30. Used up; consumed

33. The opposite of **no**

35. I have a beautiful flower _____ in my front yard.

INDEX OF KEY WORDS AND PHRASES

Words in blue are on the Academic Word List (AWL), Coxhead (2000). The AWL is a list of the 570 highest-frequency academic word families that regularly appear in academic texts. The list was compiled by researcher Averil Coxhead from a corpus of 3.5 million words.

INDEX OF KEY WORDS AND PHRASES

SKILLS INDEX

LISTENING/SPEAKING

Discussion, 2, 16–17, 21, 34, 40–41, 56, 64, 77, 96, 122, 137–138, 155, 158, 215, 222, 238

Group activities, 2, 17, 20, 21, 34, 40–41, 56, 64, 65, 77, 115, 137–138, 142, 155, 158, 215, 216, 222, 238

Interviewing, 17, 35, 58, 115, 216

Partner activities, 17, 35, 58, 80, 122

Reporting, 65

Surveys, 21, 40–41, 58, 80, 142, 179

READING

Charts, 37, 156, 157, 238

Critical thinking strategies, 13, 30–31, 52–53, 73–74, 92, 109–110, 133–134, 153–154, 173, 194–195, 211–212, 233–234

Details, 7, 25, 45–46, 69, 86, 104, 126, 147, 167, 189, 206–207, 226

Dictionary skills, 11–12, 28–29, 50–52, 72–73, 90–91, 107–108, 131–132, 151–152, 171–172, 192–193, 210–211, 231–233

Follow-up activities, 17, 34–38, 56–58, 77–80, 96, 113–115, 137–138, 156–158, 177–179, 198, 216, 239–240

Main ideas, 7, 24, 45, 68, 85, 104, 126, 147, 166, 189, 206, 226

Maps, 79–80, 235

Prereading preparation, 2, 40–41, 64–65, 82, 99–101, 122–123, 141–143, 161–162, 186–187, 201–202, 220–222

Reading analysis, 8–11, 26–28, 47–49, 70–71, 87–90, 105–107, 128–130, 149–150, 169–171, 191–192, 208–209, 228–230

Self-evaluation of reading strategies, 57, 113–114, 177–178, 239

Statement evaluation, 8, 26, 47, 70, 87, 105, 128, 148, 168, 190, 207, 227

Summarizing, 7, 25, 46, 69, 86, 105, 126, 148, 168, 190, 207, 227

Thesaurus, 30, 73, 91

Word link, 132

Word partnerships, 12, 30, 52, 109, 132, 152, 172, 193, 211, 344

TEST-TAKING SKILLS

Cloze quizzes, 18–19, 38–39, 59–60, 80–81, 97–98, 116–117, 139–140, 159–160, 180–181, 199–200, 217–219, 241–242

Matching, 240

Multiple-choice questions, 8–9, 10–11, 26–28, 47–48, 49, 70–71, 87–90, 105–107, 128–129, 130, 149–150, 169–171, 191–192, 208, 209, 228–229, 230

Short-answer questions, 9, 10–11, 13, 16, 21, 27, 28, 30–31, 33, 36–38, 47, 48, 49, 70, 71, 78–80, 88, 89, 92, 95, 106, 109–110, 129–130, 133–134, 136–137, 142–143, 149, 150, 153–154, 156, 157, 161–162, 169, 170, 173, 175–176, 186–187, 191, 194–195, 197, 202, 208–209, 211–212, 228, 229–230, 233–234, 237

True, false, or inference questions, 8, 26, 87, 105, 128, 168, 190, 227

True, false, or not mentioned questions, 47, 70, 148

True, false, or opinion questions, 207

TOPICS

VIEWING

WRITING

SKILLS INDEX